Lizzie Doten

Poems of Progress

Lizzie Doten

Poems of Progress

ISBN/EAN: 9783744705523

Printed in Europe, USA, Canada, Australia, Japan

Cover: Foto ©Thomas Meinert / pixelio.de

More available books at **www.hansebooks.com**

POEMS

OF

PROGRESS.

BY

LIZZIE DOTEN.

"If an offence come out of the Truth, better is it that the offence come, than the Truth be concealed." JEROME.

"Stand out of my sunshine." DIOGENES OF SINOPE.

BOSTON:
WILLIAM WHITE AND COMPANY,
BANNER OF LIGHT OFFICE,
158 WASHINGTON STREET.
NEW YORK AGENTS—THE AMERICAN NEWS COMPANY,
119 NASSAU STREET.
1871.

CONTENTS.

	PAGE
✓ DECLARATION OF FAITH (PREFATORY).	5
THE CHEMISTRY OF CHARACTER.	11
LET THY KINGDOM COME.	14
THE SPIRIT OF NATURE.	17
MARGERY MILLER.	20
THE LAW OF LIFE.	26
A RESPECTABLE LIE.	33
THE RAINBOW BRIDGE.	38
REST THOU IN PEACE.	42
ANGEL LILY.	44
THE ALL IN ALL.	48
"ECCE HOMO."	50
PETER McGUIRE; OR, NATURE AND GRACE.	56
HYMN OF THE ANGELS.	62
GONE HOME.	64
THE CRY OF THE DESOLATE.	66
THE SPIRIT-MOTHER.	69
FACE THE SUNSHINE.	77
HESTER VAUGHN.	83
SONG OF THE SPIRIT CHILDREN.	87
HE GIVETH HIS BELOVED SLEEP.	90
THE FAMISHED HEART.	92
✓ THE TRIUMPH OF LIFE.	99
REFORMERS.	102
MR. DE SPLAE.	105

CONTENTS.

	PAGE
WILL IT PAY?	109
THE LIVING WORD.	114
HYMN TO THE SUN.	119
GREATHEART AND GIANT DESPAIR.	123
"THE ORACLE."	128
MY ANGEL.	135
THE ANGEL OF HEALING.	139
TRUTH TRIUMPHANT.	143
GOOD IN ALL.	147
JOHN ENDICOTT.	153
THE TRIUMPH OF FREEDOM.	157
OUR SOLDIERS' GRAVES.	164
OUTWARD BOUND.	166
THE WANDERER'S WELCOME HOME.	170
LABOR AND WAIT.	174
FRAE RHYMING ROBIN.	176
AN ELEGY ON THE DEVIL.	181
FRATERNITY.	185
OWEENA.	190
GONE IS GONE, AND DEAD IS DEAD.	195
THE SPIRIT TEACHER.	198
LITTLE NELL.	203
THE SOUL'S DESTINY.	206
GUARDIAN ANGELS.	208
NEARER TO THEE.	211
THE SACRAMENT.	213
THE GOOD TIME NOW.	217
LIFE'S MYSTERIES.	221
A WOODLAND IDYL.	225
JUBILATE.	229
THE DIVINE IDEA.	231
THE PYRAMIDS.	235
THE INNER MYSTERY.	237

DECLARATION OF FAITH.

DOUBTLESS many who take up this book, and glance carelessly at its pages, will exclaim, "What! more Spiritualism!" To which remark I answer, yes, more Spiritualism, an unequivocal, undisguised, positive Spiritualism — confirmed by many years of careful observation, study, and experience, and of which this book is the legitimate outgrowth. Eight years have elapsed since my first volume — "Poems from the Inner Life" — was given to the world (to the Preface of which I now refer for any explanation concerning my mediumship). During that interval of time, the ranks of the believers in Spiritualism have steadily increased in numbers, its phenomena, presenting an array of well-established facts, have challenged the investigation of some of the first scientific minds of the age, and its philosophy has done more towards liberating the human mind from the thraldom of old superstitions and creeds than any other form of faith which has arisen for centuries. But as yet, it has not secured that prestige of popularity and respectability which the combined influence of age, wealth, and organized action ever afforded. Consequently, those who are "named by its name" must be prepared to meet the anathemas of religious bigots — the lofty scorn of those who are wise in their own conceit — the scurrilous attacks of those who would divert attention from their own infamy and the petty irritations of a numerous pack who follow at the heels of every new movement, and ever distinguish themselves by noise rather than by knowledge. As a participant in this great movement, I have found such attacks to be helps rather than hinderances to my progress, inasmuch as I have been enabled to define my own positive and affirmative position more clearly from the negations of the opposers of Spiritualism.

We are told that "it is not a Religion." But after a long and careful study of the past and present, I have yet to find any phase of faith, which, in its very inception has commenced so directly at the root of all necessary reform, viz., the purification and harmonious development of the human body. This primary and fundamental truth has been taken as a starting-point — it has been enunciated from the spirit world — repeated by the inspirational speakers — has been interwoven with all the spiritualistic literature, and has found a practical application in the Children's Lyceums. The religion that teaches, "Take care of the soul, and let the body take care of itself," will inevitably defeat its own purposes, and has already been taught long enough for us to know that it is a failure. No other form of faith ever brought the spiritual world so near, *as to banish its supernatural character, and place it within the province of natural law.* No other form of faith has *illustrated* the fact *so clearly*, that just as we go out of this world, so do we enter upon the next, thereby presenting a more rational incentive to endeavor, than the rewards of Heaven or the punishments of Hell; and no other form of faith has so effectually dissipated the idea of an inane and purposeless life in the future, and given to the angels a more exalted employment than "loafing around the throne." It also teaches that mediumship, under proper circumstances, is a *healthy, harmonious, and normal development of human nature*, and that communion with the spiritual world is not interdicted, and no more impossible than any other attainment that lies in the direct line of natural law, human progress, and scientific investigation. This to me, and to those who have accepted Spiritualism thoughtfully and sincerely, makes it *a religion indeed*, and the positive assertions of any number of intellectual or religious "authorities" to the contrary cannot make it otherwise.

We have been told again and again, that "Spiritualism is

Supernaturalism," that we believe in miracles, which are contrary to the "methods" of God's government. We have denied this repeatedly, assuming that we ourselves had the best right to say what we did believe; but our denial has not been accepted, and the reason is obvious. Any number of scholastic discourses, elaborately written essays, and eloquent appeals to popular prejudice, would lose their pith and marrow, and be found wanting, if this false predicate, this fabricated nucleus for their logic should be disallowed.

Again, we are told that "Spiritualism is not Science;" to which we reply, that Spiritualism has presented facts and phenomena which the later discoveries in Science are tending both to explain and substantiate. It has been demonstrated that it is not the eye that sees, the ear that hears, or the nerves that feel, but each of these avenues of sense serves to convey the vibrations of the surrounding "ether" to the central consciousness, which alone is possessed of the power of perception. Since this is so, who shall dare place a limit to the possibilities of that consciousness, of which so little is definitely known? Or why should any man prescribe, as a standard for all others, the limitations of his own feeble consciousness. A modern reasoner tells us that "if the bodily ear receives vibrations from one atmosphere, it *cannot* receive them from another, and no fiction of an inner ear can give genuineness to voices and whispers of a spiritual tongue." Since, however, it is not the outer ear, but the inner consciousness, that hears, a quickening of its perceptions will allow it to catch the vibrations from another atmosphere, and Spiritualism demonstrates, by indisputable facts, that this is so. Also, that this is not an *abnormal* condition, but *perfectly legitimate* to certain states of the inner consciousness.

The revelations of the spectroscope, and the investigations of some of the greatest scientific minds of the present day, have determined the existence of a higher scale of vibrations than those which fall within the ordinary range of human vision. All the objects and forms of life comprehended in that scale, although so closely blended and interwoven with the vibrations of our own plane of existence, are lost to our dull perceptions, unless, through some physical or mental condition, there is a quickening of our inner consciousness. When this comes, as it has again and again to many, we have revelations from the "*spirit world*," which is, after all, but a finer *material* world, as real, as substantial, as objective, and as directly within the province of universal law, as that which we now inhabit. That we should be made sensibly aware of this higher life, under certain legitimate conditions, is perfectly *natural*. Indeed, it would be strange, with the uniformity of succession and development which pervades all things, if we were not. It is not a world that is *possible*, but *actual*, not one that *might* be, but *is*.

In this matter, intelligent Spiritualists range themselves side by side with those of whom Professor Tyndall has said, "You never hear the really philosophical defenders of the doctrine of uniformity speaking of *impossibilities* in nature. They best know that questions offer themselves to thought, which Science, as now prosecuted, has not even the tendency to solve. They keep such questions open, *and will not tolerate any unlawful limitations of the horizon of their souls*." However weak and imperfect our spiritual vision may be at present, we shall use each and every opportunity of obtaining all the information that is possible, either from this world or the next. The report of the committee chosen by the London Dialectical Society, to investigate the subject of Spiritualism, "bears strong testimony in favor of the reality of the manifestations,' and is a step in the right direction. All we ask of our opponents, is fair treatment and an unprejudiced consideration of the facts and phenomena which Spiritualism presents. We do not fear as to the result.

But the objection which is most frequently urged against Spiritualism is, that "it is immoral in its tendencies." In my anxiety to prove all things, I have also taken this matter into careful consideration, and diligently compared the annals of crime in the so-called Christian church with those of Spiritualism. For several years I have collected the items from the daily newspapers, that I might have them for future reference, and in due time come to a just and impartial conclusion. As I write, that record of ministerial delinquency, ecclesiastical abominations, and human frailty, lies before me. Where I have found one spiritual sheep that has gone astray, I have found ninety and nine of the Shepherds in Israel in great need of repentance. Let the church cleanse her own Augean stables before she utters one word in relation to the immoralities of Spiritualism. Casting stones and calling hard names will not profit either party. It is neither Christianity nor Spiritualism that is responsible for these immoralities, but *poor human nature*. The remedy lies not in creeds or forms of faith, but in the growth of Truth in the Understanding, and Love in the heart. Not as a Spiritualist, but as a child of humanity, do I hope that the entire world may yet have a moral standard, harmonious with the laws of God and Nature, and consistent with the highest good of the individual and society.

Having, from inclination and a sense of duty to my kindred in the faith, pursued the subject thus far, the "Spirit moves me" to present, in conclusion, a few quotations which require neither comment nor explanation.

"If we are *wise* we shall sit down upon the brink and content ourselves with saying what the spiritual world *is not* and *cannot be*. * * The soul *must* be entirely ignorant of the second body until it has ceased to use the first. * * The new organs may be, all correspond in intention and effect to the present ones; but we say that *they do not yet exist. They cannot exist;* the ground is pre-occupied." *John Weiss*,
Unitarian Monthly Journal, May, 1866.

"Moreover, the satellites of Jupiter are invisible to the naked eye, and therefore can exercise no influence over the Earth, and therefore would be useless, and therefore *do not exist*." *Francesco Sizzi*, Times of Galileo.

"If the Spiritualists would secure the favor of *sensible people* they must let them see that they are not at war with good sense. * * It were better that very sacred and dear beliefs

should go, than that this enemy of all rational belief should remain. Let us prefer to have *no* other world, than to have another world full of teasing, troublesome, meddlesome beings, who interfere with the rational order of the world we dwell in." *O. B. Frothingham,*
" The Index," July 8, 1871.

" If the new planets were acknowledged, what a chaos would ensue ! " * * " I will never concede his four new planets to that Italian, though I die for it."
Martin Horky, Times of Galileo.

" O my beloved Kepler ! How I wish we could have one good laugh together! Here, at Padua, is the principal Professor of Philosophy, whom I have repeatedly and urgently requested to look at the moon and planets through my telescope, which he pertinaciously refuses to do ! Why, my dear Kepler, are you not here ? What shouts of laughter we should have at *all this solemn folly !* "
Letter from Galileo to John Kepler.

POEMS OF PROGRESS.

THE CHEMISTRY OF CHARACTER.

John, and Peter, and Robert, and Paul,
God in his wisdom created them all.
John was a statesman, and Peter a slave,
Robert a preacher, and Paul — was a knave.
Evil or good as the case might be,
White, or colored, or bond, or free —
John, and Peter, and Robert, and Paul,
God in his wisdom created them all.

Out of earth's elements, mingled with flame,
Out of life's compounds of glory and shame,
Fashioned and shaped by no will of their own,
And helplessly into life's history thrown;
Born by the law that compels men to be,
Born to conditions they could not foresee,
John, and Peter, and Robert, and Paul,
God in his wisdom created them all.

John was the head and the heart of his State,
Was trusted and honored, was noble and great.
Peter was made 'neath life's burdens to groan,
And never once dreamed that his soul was his own.
Robert great glory and honor received,
For zealously preaching what no one believed;
While Paul, of the pleasures of sin took his fill,
And gave up his life to the service of ill.

It chanced that these men, in their passing away
From earth and its conflicts, all died the same day.
John was mourned through the length and the breadth of the land —
Peter fell 'neath the lash in a merciless hand —
Robert died with the praise of the Lord on his tongue —
While Paul was convicted of murder, and hung.
John, and Peter, and Robert, and Paul,
The purpose of life was fulfilled in them all.

Men said of the Statesman — "How noble and brave!"
But of Peter, alas! — "he was only a Slave."
Of Robert — "'Tis well with his soul — it is well;"
While Paul they consigned to the torments of hell.

Born by one law through all Nature the same,
What made them differ? and *who* was to blame?
John, and Peter, and Robert, and Paul,
God in his wisdom created them all.

Out in that region of infinite light,
Where the soul of the black man is pure as the white —
Out where the spirit, through sorrow made wise,
No longer resorts to deception and lies —
Out where the flesh can no longer control
The freedom and faith of the God-given soul —
Who shall determine what change may befall
John, and Peter, and Robert, and Paul?

John may in wisdom and goodness increase —
Peter rejoice in an infinite peace —
Robert may learn that the truths of the Lord
Are more in the spirit, and less in the word —
And Paul may be blest with a holier birth
Than the passions of man had allowed him on earth.
John, and Peter, and Robert, and Paul,
God in his wisdom will care for them all.

LET THY KINGDOM COME.

The peaceful night, "the stilly night,"
   Came down on wings of purple gloom,
And with her eyes of starry light,
   Looked through the darkness of my room;
Peace was the pillow for my head,
While angels watched around my bed.

Freed from a weight of cumbering care,
   My earnest spirit seemed to rise,
And on the wings of faith and prayer,
   I sought the gates of Paradise;
Like priceless pearls I saw them gleam,
As in the Revelator's dream.

O, holy, holy was the song
   Of blessed spirits echoing thence,
So soft and clear it swept along,
   It ravished all my soul and sense;
Close to those gates of light I crept,
And like a homeless orphan wept.

The white-robed angels went and came —
   The white-robed angels saw me there —
And one, in our dear Father's name,
   Came at my spirit's voiceless prayer.
"Dear child," he said, "why dost thou wait
With weeping at the heavenly gate?"

"O, weary are my feet," I cried,
   "With wandering o'er the earthly way;
Lo, all my hopes hang crucified,
   And all my idols turn to clay;
Far distant now the Father seems,
And heaven comes only in my dreams."

He laid his hand upon my head,
   "And tenderly the angel smiled.
"Thy Father knows thy need," he said,
   "And he will aid his suffering child.
Return unto thine earthly home —
His kingdom yet shall surely come."

Obedient at the word I turned,
   And sought mine earthly home once more,
While all my soul within me burned,
   With joy I never knew before;
For that blest vision of the night
Had filled me with celestial light.

Still o'er my life its glories stream,
    The solace of my lonely hours,
Fair as the sunset's golden gleam,
    And lovely as the bloom of flowers;
A sweet assurance, calm and deep,
Which treasured in my soul I keep.

Henceforth I wait with anxious eyes,
    Until the shadows flee away,
To see the morning star arise,
    Which ushers in that glorious day.
Be patient, O my heart! be still
Till time the promise shall fulfill.

THE SPIRIT OF NATURE.

"The bond which unites the human to the divine is Love, and Love is the longing of the Soul for Beauty; the inextinguishable desire which like feels for like, which the divinity within us feels for the divinity revealed to us in Beauty. Beauty is Truth." — PLATO.

I HAVE come from the heart of all natural things,
Whose life from the Soul of the Beautiful springs;
You shall hear the sweet waving of corn in my
    voice,
And the musical whisper of leaves that rejoice,
For my lips have been touched by the spirit of
    prayer,
Which lingers unseen in the soft summer air;
And the smile of the sunshine that brightens the
    skies,
Hath left a glad ray of its light in my eyes.

On the sea-beaten shore — 'mid the dwellings of
    men —
In the field, or the forest, or wild mountain glen;

Wherever the grass or a daisy could spring,
Or the musical laughter of childhood could ring;
Wherever a swallow could build 'neath the eaves,
Or a squirrel could hide in his covert of leaves,
I have felt the sweet presence, and heard the low
  call,
Of the Spirit of Nature, which quickens us all.

Grown weary and worn with the conflict of creeds,
I had sought a new faith for the soul with its needs,
When the love of the Beautiful guided my feet
Through a leafy arcade to a sylvan retreat,
Where the oriole sung in the branches above,
And the wild roses burned with their blushes of
  love,
And the purple-fringed aster, and bright golden-
  rod,
Like jewels of beauty adorned the green sod.

O, how blessèd to feel from the care-laden heart
All the sorrows and woes that oppressed it depart,
And to lay the tired head, with its achings, to rest
On the heart of all others that loves it the best;
O, thus is it ever, when, wearied, we yearn
To the bosom of Nature and Truth to return,
And life blossoms forth into beauty anew,
As we learn to repose in the Simple and True.

No longer with self or with Nature at strife,
The soul feels the presence of Infinite Life;
And the voice of a child, or the hum of a bee —
The somnolent roll of the deep-heaving sea —
The mountains uprising in grandeur and might —
The stars that look forth from the depths of the
    night —
All speak in one language, persuasive and clear,
To him who in spirit is waiting to hear.

There is something in Nature beyond our control,
That is tenderly winning the love of each soul;
We shall linger no longer in darkness and doubt,
When the Beauty within meets the Beauty with-
    out.
Sweet Spirit of Nature! wherever thou art,
O, fold us like children, close, close to thy heart;
Till we learn that thy bosom is Truth's hallowed
    shrine,
And the Soul of the Beautiful is — the Divine.

MARGERY MILLER.

Old Margery Miller sat alone,
One Christmas eve, by her poor hearthstone,
Where dimly the fading firelight shone.

Her brow was furrowed with signs of care,
Her lips moved gently, as if in prayer —
For O, life's burden was hard to bear.
  Poor old Margery Miller!
   Sitting alone,
   Unsought, unknown,
Her friends, like the birds of summer had flown.

Full eighty summers had swiftly sped,
Full eighty winters their snows had shed,
With silver-sheen, on her aged head.

One by one had her loved ones died —
One by one had they left her side —
Fading like flowers in their summer pride.

Poor old Margery Miller!
    Sitting alone,
      Unsought, unknown,
Had God forgotten *she* was his own?

No castle was hers with a spacious lawn;
Her poor old hut was the proud man's scorn;
Yet Margery Miller was nobly born.

A brother she had, who once wore a crown,
Whose deeds of greatness and high renown
From age to age had been handed down.
    Poor old Margery Miller!
      Sitting alone,
        Unsought, unknown,
Where was her kingdom, her crown or throne?

Margery Miller, a child of God,
Meekly and bravely life's path had trod,
Nor deemed affliction a "chastening rod."

Her brother, Jesus, who went before,
A crown of thorns in his meekness wore,
And what, poor soul! could *she* hope for more?
    Poor old Margery Miller!
      Sitting alone,
        Unsought, unknown,
Strange that her heart had not turned to stone!

Ay, there she sat, on that Christmas eve,
Seeking some dream of the past to weave,
Patiently striving not to grieve.

O, for those long, long eighty years,
How had she struggled with doubts and fears,
Shedding in secret unnumbered tears!
      Poor old Margery Miller!
        Sitting alone,
          Unsought, unknown,
How *could* she stifle her sad heart's moan?

Soft on her ear fell the Christmas chimes,
Bringing the thought of the dear old times,
Like birds that sing of far distant climes.

Then swelled the flood of her pent-up grief—
Swayed like a reed in the tempest brief,
Her bowed form shook like an aspen leaf.
      Poor old Margery Miller!
        Sitting alone,
          Unsought, unknown,
How heavy the burden of life had grown!

"O God!" she cried, "I am lonely here,
Bereft of all that my heart holds dear;
Yet Thou dost never refuse to hear.

"O, if the dead were allowed to speak!
Could I only look on their faces meek,
How it would strengthen my heart so weak!"
      Poor old Margery Miller!
        Sitting alone,
        Unsought, unknown,
What was that light which around her shone?

Dim on the hearth burned the embers red,
Yet soft and clear, on her silvered head,
A light like the sunset glow was shed.

Bright blossoms fell on the cottage floor,
"Mother" was whispered, as oft before,
And long-lost faces gleamed forth once more.
      Poor old Margery Miller!
        No longer alone,
        Unsought, unknown,
How light the burden of life had grown!

She lifted her withered hands on high,
And uttered the eager, earnest cry,
"God of all mercy! now let me die.

"Beautiful Angels, fair and bright,
Holding the *hem* of your garments white,
Let me go forth to the world of light."

Poor old Margery Miller!
So earnest grown!
Was she left alone?
His humble child did the Lord disown?

O, sweet was the sound of the Christmas bell,
As its musical changes rose and fell,
With a low refrain or a solemn swell.

But sweeter by far was the blessèd strain,
That soothed old Margery Miller's pain,
And gave her comfort and peace again.
Poor old Margery Miller!
In silence alone,
Her faith had grown;
And now the blossom had brightly blown.

Out of the glory that burned like flame,
Calmly a great white angel came —
Softly he whispered her humble name.

"Child of the highest," he gently said,
"Thy toils are ended, thy tears are shed,
And life immortal now crowns thy head."
Poor old Margery Miller!
No longer alone,
Unsought, unknown,
God *had not* forgotten she was his own.

A change o'er her pallid features passed;
She felt that her feet were nearing fast
The land of safety and peace, at last.

She faintly murmured, "God's name be blest!"
And folding her hands on her dying breast,
She calmly sank to her dreamless rest.
   Poor old Margery Miller!
    Sitting alone,
    Without one moan,
Her patient spirit at length had flown.

Next morning a stranger found her there,
Her pale hands folded as if in prayer,
Sitting so still in her old arm-chair.

He spoke — but she answered not again,
For, far away from all earthly pain,
Her voice was singing a joyful strain.
   Poor old Margery Miller!
    Her spirit had flown
    To the world unknown,
Where true hearts *never* can be alone.

THE LAW OF LIFE.

DEEPLY musing
On the many mysteries of life;
Half excusing
All man's seeming failures in the strife;
Through the city
Did I take my lonely way at night;
Filled with pity
For the miseries that met my sight,
In the faces, sickly, sad and sunken,
In the faces, meager, mean and shrunken,
Wanton, leering, passionate and drunken,
Which I saw that night,
Passing through the city —
Saw them by the street-lamps' changing light.

Burning brightly,
Looked the watching stars from heaven above;
As if lightly
They beheld these wrecks of human love.

"O, how distant,"
Said I, "are they from this earth apart!
How resistant
To the woes that rend the human heart!
Countless worlds! your radiant courses rounding,
With your light the depth of distance sounding,
Is there not some fount of love abounding?
O, thou starlit night
Brooding o'er the city!
Would that truth might as thy stars shine bright."

Very lightly
Was a woman's hand laid on my arm.
Pressing slightly —
And a voice said — striving to be calm —
"I am dying,
Slowly dying for the want of love;
Vainly trying
To believe there is a God above.
For I feel that I am sinking slowly,
Losing daily, faith and patience lowly,
Doomed to ways of sin and deeds unholy —
All the weary night,
Through this cruel city
Do I wander till the morning light.

"Hear me kindly,
For I am not what I would have been,
If most blindly
I had not been tempted unto sin.
I am lonely,
And I long to shriek in anguish wild,
O, if only
I could be once more a little child!
See! my eyes are weary-worn with weeping;
Sorrow's tide across my soul is sweeping;
God no longer holds me in his keeping —
I have prayed to-night,
Wandering through the city,
That I might not see the morning light."

Breathless, gazing
On her pallid and impassioned face,
How amazing
Was the likeness that I there could trace!
"Sister!" "Brother!"
From our lips as by one impulse broke.
Not another
Word, then, for an instant brief we spoke.
But the sweet and tender recollection
Of our childhood, with its fond affection,
And at last, the broken, lost connection,

Came afresh that night,
Standing in the city
Underneath the street-lamps' changing light.

Pale and slender,
Like a lily did she bow her head.
Low and tender
Was the earnest tone in which she said —
"O, my brother!
Tell me of our father." — "He is dead."
"And our mother?"
"And she, also, rests in peace," I said.
Only to my grievous words replying,
By a long-drawn, deep and painful sighing,
Sinking downward, as if crushed and dying,
Did she seem that night,
Standing in the city
Underneath the street-lamps' changing light.

Wherefore should I
Thrust her from my guilty heart away?
Ah, how could I!
Whatsoe'er the *righteous* world might say —
She, my sister,
One who shared in mine own life a part —
Nay, I kissed her,
And upraised her to a brother's heart.

And I said, "Henceforth we will not sever,
But with faith and patience failing never,
We will work for truth and right forever.
　　Ministers of light,
　　　Watching o'er the city!
Guide! O, guide our erring feet aright!"

　　　Gently o'er us
Came a breath of warm and balmy air,
　　And before us
Stood a man with silvery, flowing hair.
　　How appearing
From the murky gloom that round us fell,
　　Mild and cheering
In his presence, I could never tell.
But I say with solemn asservation,
That it was no fanciful creation,
Bearing to this life no true relation,
　　　Which we saw that night,
　　　Standing in the city,
Underneath the street-lamps' changing light.

　　"Children!" said he,
"One of life's great lessons you are taught;
　　Be then ready
To apply the teaching as you ought.

All are brothers —
All are sisters in this lower life.
Many others
Make sad failures in the weary strife;
But each failure is a grand expression
Of the law which underlies progression,
Which will raise the soul above transgression.
Yea, this very night,
All throughout this city,
Every soul is striving toward the light."

"Bruised and broken,
Many hearts in patient sorrow wait,
To hear spoken
Words of love, which often come too late.
Lift their crosses,
And their sins — the heaviest load of all —
Bear their losses,
And be patient with them when they fall."
Then he vanished, as the shadows parted,
Leaving us alone, but hopeful hearted,
Gazing into space where he departed
From our wondering sight,
In that mazy city —
Vanished in the shadows of the night.

Sacred presence!
Dwelling just beyond our mortal sense,
Through thine essence,
Fill our beings with a life intense.
By creation
Man fulfills a destiny sublime,
And salvation
Comes to each in its appointed time.
In that region of celestial splendor,
Where the angel-faces look so tender,
Human weakness needeth no defender.
In the perfect light
Of the heavenly city,
Souls can read the law of life aright.

A RESPECTABLE LIE.

"A RESPECTABLE lie, sir! Pray what do you mean?
   Why the term in *itself* is a plain contradiction.
A lie is a *lie*, and deserves no respect,
   But merciless judgment, and speedy conviction.
It springs from corruption, is servile and mean,
   An evil conception, a coward's invention,
And whether direct, or but simply implied,
   Has naught but deceit for its end and intention."

Ah, yes! very well! So *good morals* would teach;
   But *facts* are the *most* stubborn things in existence,
And *they* tend to show that *great* lies win respect,
   And hold their position with wondrous persistence.
The *small* lies, the *white* lies, the lies *feebly told*,
   The world will condemn both in spirit and letter;
But the *great, bloated* lies will be held in respect,
   And the *larger* and *older* a lie is, the better.

A respectable lie, from a *popular* man,
   On a *popular* theme, never taxes endurance;
And the pure, golden coin of *un*popular *truth*,
   Is often *refused* for the *brass of assurance.*
You may dare all the laws of the land to defy,
   And bear to the truth the most shameless relation,
But never attack *a respectable lie*,
   If you value a name, or a good reputation.

A lie well established, and hoary with age,
   Resists the assaults of the boldest seceder;
While he is accounted the greatest of saints,
   Who silences reason and follows the leader.
Whenever a mortal has *dared* to be wise,
   And seize upon Truth, as the soul's "Magna Charta,"
He always has won from the lovers of lies,
   The name of a fool, or the fate of a martyr.

There are popular lies, and political lies,
   And "lies that stick fast between buying and selling,"
And lies of politeness — conventional lies —
   (Which scarcely are reckoned as such in the telling.)

There are lies of sheer malice, and slanderous lies,
  From those who delight to peck filth like a pigeon;
But the *oldest* and far *most respectable* lies,
  Are those that are told in the name of Religion.

Theology sits like a tyrant enthroned,
  A system *per se* with a fixed nomenclature,
Derived from strange doctrines, and dogmas, and creeds,
  At war with man's reason, with God and with Nature;
And he who subscribes to the popular faith,
  Never questions the fact of divine inspiration,
But holds to the Bible as absolute truth,
  From Genesis through to St. John's Revelation.

We mock at the Catholic bigots at Rome,
  Who strive with their dogmas man's reason to fetter;
But we turn to the Protestant bigots at home,
  And we find that their dogmas are scarce a whit better.

We are called to believe in the wrath of the
    Lord —
In endless damnation, and torments infernal;
While around and above us, the Infinite Truth,
    Scarce heeded or heard, speaks sublime and
    eternal.

It is sad — but the day-star is shining on high,
    And Science comes in with her conquering
    legions;
And ev'ry respectable, time-honored lie,
    Will fly from her face to the mythical regions.
The soul shall no longer with terror behold
    The red waves of wrath that leap up to engulf
    her,
For Science ignores the existence of hell,
    And chemistry finds better uses for sulphur.

We may dare to repose in the beautiful faith,
    That an Infinite Life is the source of all
    being;
And though we must strive with delusion and
    Death,
    We can trust to a love and a wisdom all-
    seeing;

We may dare in the strength of the soul to arise,
    And walk where our feet shall not stumble or falter;
And, freed from the bondage of time-honored lies,
    To lay all we have on the Truth's sacred altar.

THE RAINBOW BRIDGE.

'Twas a faith that was held by the Northmen
    bold,
  In the ages long, long ago,
That the river of death, so dark and cold,
  Was spanned by a radiant bow;
A rainbow bridge to the blest abode
  Of the strong Gods — free from ill,
Where the beautiful Urda fountain flowed,
  Near the ash tree Igdrasill.

They held that when, in life's weary march,
  They should come to that river wide,
They would set their feet on the shining arch,
  And would pass to the other side.
And they said that the Gods and the Heroes
    crossed
  That bridge from the world of light,
To strengthen the Soul when its hope seemed lost,
  In the conflict for the right.

O, beautiful faith of the grand old past!
   So simple, yet so sublime,
A light from that rainbow bridge is cast
   Far down o'er the tide of time.
We raise our eyes, and we see above,
   The souls in their homeward march;
They wave their hands and they smile in love,
   From the height of the rainbow arch.

We know they will drink from the fountain pure
   That springs by the Tree of Life,
We know that their spirits will rest secure
   From the tempests of human strife;
So we fold our hands, and we close our eyes,
   And we strive to forget our pain,
Lest the weak and the selfish wish should rise,
   To ask for them back again.

The swelling tide of our grief we stay,
   While our warm hearts fondly yearn,
And we ask if over that shining way
   They shall nevermore return.
O, we oft forget that our lonely hours
   Are known to the souls we love,
And they strew the path of our life with flowers,
   From that rainbow arch above.

We hear them call, and their voices sweet
    Float down from that bridge of light,
Where the gold and crimson and azure meet,
    And mingle their glories bright.
We hear them call, and the soul replies,
    From the depths of the life below,
And we strive on the wings of faith to rise
    To the height of that radiant bow.

Like the crystal ladder that Jacob saw,
    Is that beautiful vision given,
The weary pilgrims of earth to draw
    To the life of their native heaven.
For 'tis better that souls should upward tend,
    And strive for the victor's crown,
Than to ask the angels their help to lend,
    And come to man's weakness down.

That rainbow bridge in the crystal dome,
    O'er a swiftly flowing tide,
Is the shining way to the spirit home,
    That lies on the other side.
To man is the tempest cloud below,
    And the storm wind's fatal breath,
But for those who cross o'er that shining bow,
    There is no more pain nor death.

O, fair and bright does that archway stand,
  Through the silent lapse of years,
Fashioned and reared by no human hand,
  From the sunshine of love and tears.
Sweet spirits, our footsteps are nearing fast
  The light of the shining shore;
We shall cross that rainbow bridge at last,
  And greet you in joy once more.

REST THOU IN PEACE.

> "And the token that the angel gave her, that he was a true messenger, was an arrow, with a point sharpened with Love, let easily into her heart, which by degrees wrought so effectually with her, that at the time appointed she must be gone."
> PILGRIM'S PROGRESS.

REST thou in peace! Beneath the sheltering sod
  There is a lowly door, a narrow way,
That leadeth to the Paradise of God;
  There, weary pilgrim, let thy wanderings stay.

Rest thou in peace! We would not call thee back
  To know the grief that comes with riper years,
To tread in sorrow all Life's thorny track,
  And drain with us the bitter cup of tears.

Rest thou in peace! With chastened hearts we bow,
  And pour for thee a low and solemn strain;
Thy voice shall chant the hymns of Zion now,
  But it shall mingle not with ours again.

Rest thou in peace! Not in the silent grave —
　Thy spirit heard the summons from above,
And blessed the token that the angel gave —
　An arrow, sharpened — but with tenderest love.

Rest thou in peace! With blessings on thy head,
　Pass to the land where sinless spirits dwell —
Gone, but not lost! — We will not call thee *dead* —
　The angels claimed thee! Dear one — Fare-thee-well.

ANGEL LILY.

Of all the flowers that greet the light,
   Or open 'neath the summer's sun,
With fragrance sweet, and beauty bright,
   The Lily is the fairest one,
And in its incense-cup there lies
A perfume, as from Paradise.

O, once there lived a fair, sweet child,
   And Lily was her gentle name;
As beautiful and meekly mild,
   As if from Heaven's pure life she came—
A breathing psalm, a living prayer,
To make men think of worlds more fair.

O, there was sunshine in her smile,
   And music in her dancing feet,
And every tender, artless wile,
   Made her dear presence seem more sweet;
But ever in her childish play,
A strange, unfathomed mystery lay.

Her playmates — well, we could not see
    That which our darling Lily saw —
But often in her childish glee,
    She filled our loving hearts with awe,
When, pointing to the viewless air,
She told us of the Angels there.

"O, very beautiful!" she said,
    "And very gentle are they all;
At night they watch around my bed,
    And always answer to my call.
I asked to go with them one day,
But a tall angel told me nay."

Yes — the "tall Angel" told her nay,
    But it was only for a time;
We knew our Lily could not stay
    Long in this uncongenial clime.
Into their home of love and light
The Angels led her from our sight.

They led her from the earth away,
    Into the blesséd "summer-land,"
Leaving to us her form of clay,
    With budding lilies in the hand;
An emblem of her life, to be
Unfolded in Eternity.

O, though there falls a gloom like night
  From Sorrow's overshadowing wing,
How often does returning light
  A ray of heavenly brightness bring,
And problems that were dark before
Can vex the soul with doubt no more.

Beneath that heavy cloud we stood,
  Through which no ray of gladness stole,
But well we knew that Sorrow's flood
  Would cleanse and purify the soul;
And when its ministry should cease,
Our lives would blossom fair with peace.

One evening, when the summer moon
  With silver radiance filled the sky,
And through the fragrant flowers of June
  The balmy breeze sighed dreamily,
With spirits calm and reconciled,
We talked of our dear Angel child.

We spoke of her we loved so well,
  As one who only went before —
When lo! just where the moonlight fell
  With mellow lustre on the floor,
We saw our own sweet darling stand,
With half-blown lilies in her hand.

She seemed more beautiful and fair
    Than when a simple child of earth;
The golden glory in her hair
    Betokened her celestial birth;
But as she sweetly looked and smiled,
We knew she was our own dear child.

O, strange to say! we did not start,
    We did not even wildly weep,
For each had schooled the wayward heart
    The law of perfect peace to keep —
And deep as Love's unfathomed sea
Had been our faith that *this would be.*

O; shall we tell those moments o'er —
    And all her words of love repeat —
And say how, through Time's open door
    She glided in with noiseless feet?
Nay, rather let us purely hold
Such things too sacred to be told.

Enough to say we wait our time,
    With heaven's own sunshine in the heart,
Rejoicing in the faith sublime,
    That those who love *can never part,*
And wheresoe'er the soul may dwell,
That God will order all things well.

THE ALL IN ALL.

How beautiful the roses bloom
Around the portals of the tomb!
How fair the meek white lilies grow
From elements of death below!
How tender and serenely bright
The stars light up the depths of night!

Thus beauty unto ruin clings,
And light from deepest darkness springs;
The Soul its noblest strength must gain
Through ministries of grief and pain;
Great victories only come through strife,
And death is but the gate of life.

The ocean waves that darkly flow,
Sweep over priceless pearls below;
The tempest cloud, when wild winds rest,
Builds up the rainbow on its breast,
And truths, unseen when all is bright,
Shine like the stars in sorrow's night.

THE ALL IN ALL.

O Thou, in whom the vine bears fruit!
In whom the violets take their root,
For Thee the summer roses blow;
For Thee the fair white lilies grow;
And from Thine all-sustaining heart
The Soul's immortal currents start.

O, when the circle, made complete,
Shall in thy boundless being meet,
We feel, we know, that we shall be
Made perfect in our love to Thee;
That good will triumph in that hour,
And weakness be exchanged for power.

"ECCE HOMO."

" When the Son of Man cometh, shall he find faith in the earth?"
LUKE xviii. 8.

THE merry Christmas time,
With song and silvery chime,
  Had come at last;
And brightly glowed each hearth,
While winter, o'er the earth,
  Its snows had cast.
High in the old cathedral tower,
  The ponderous bell majestic swung,
And with its voice of solemn power
  A summons to the people rung.

Then, forth from lowly walls,
And proud, ancestral halls,
  Came rich and poor,
And faces wreathed with smiles
Thronged the cathedral aisles
  As ne'er before.

Rich silks trailed o'er the marble pave,
  And costly jewels glittered bright,
For groined arch and spacious nave
  Were radiant with excess of light.

 The deep-toned organ's swell
 Like billows rose and fell,
  In floods of sound;
 And the "Te Deum" rung,
 As if by angels sung,
  In space profound.
Forth the majestic anthem rolled
  In harmony complete, and then
Pealed forth the angels' song of old,
  Of "peace on earth, good will to men."

 As the full chorus ceased,
 Up rose the white-robed priest,
  With solemn air;
 With hands toward heaven outspread,
 He bowed his stately head
  In formal prayer.
Then, like some breathless, holy spell,
  Upon the hushed and reverent crowd,
A deep, impressive silence fell,
  And hands were clasped, and heads were
    bowed.

"Saviour of All!" he cried,
"Thou who wast crucified
  For sinful man!
We worship at thy feet,
For thou hast made complete
  Salvation's plan.
Come to thy people, Lord, once more,
  And let the nations hear again
The song the angels sung of yore,
  Of 'peace on earth, good will to men.'"

As if his prayer was heard,
A sudden trembling stirred
  The walls around.
The doors, wide open flung,
On ponderous hinges swung,
  With solemn sound.
And then, straight up the foot-worn aisle,
  A strange procession made its way,
In garments coarse, of simplest style,
  A strange, incongruous array.

The first, most rudely clad,
A leathern girdle had
  About him bound.
The next, in humblest guise,
Raised not his mournful eyes
  From off the ground.

And next to these the dusky browed,
   And others, flushed with sin and shame,
And women, with their faces bowed
   In deep contrition, slowly came.

   No voice was heard, or sound,
     From the vast concourse round,
       Outspreading wide.
     But onward still they passed,
     Until they gained at last
       The altar side.
Then said the lowly one, "O ye!
   Who celebrate a Saviour's birth,
Should he return again, would he
   Find faith among the sons of earth?"

   Quick, with an angry frown,
     The haughty priest looked down
       Upon the crowd.
   "Who are ye, that ye dare
     Invade this house of prayer?"
       He cried aloud.
"This temple, sacred to the Lord,
   Not thus shall be profaned by you:
Your deeds with his do not accord —
   Begone! Begone, ye vagrant crew!"

The lowly one replied,
"These, standing by my side,
  Came at my call;
Nor need they have one fear,
With me to enter here —
  God loves them all.
Thou hypocrite! thou dost reject
  Me, through thy most *unchristian creed*,
And making truth of none effect,
  Thou dost dishonor me indeed."

Around the stranger's head
A radiant halo spread
  Its glories bright;
His meek and tender face
Beamed with transcendent grace,
  And heavenly light.
There, mighty in his power for good,
  So gentle and divinely sweet,
The "Christus Consolator" stood,
  With weeping sinners at his feet.

"We must go hence," he said,
"To find the living bread.
  Come, follow me!
My Father's house above
Is full of light and love,
  And all is free."

High in the old cathedral tower,
　　The brazen bell majestic swung,
As if some strange, mysterious power
　　To sudden speech had moved its tongue.

　　　O Christ! thou friend of men!
　　　　When thou shalt come again,
　　　　　Through Truth's new birth,
　　　　May all the fruits of peace
　　　　Be found in rich increase
　　　　　Upon the earth.
Then shall the song of sweet accord,
　　Sung by the heavenly hosts of yore,
To hail the coming of their Lord,
　　Sound through the ages evermore.

PETER McGUIRE; OR, NATURE AND GRACE.

It has always been thought a most critical case,
When a man was possessed of more Nature than
 Grace;
For Theology teaches that man from the first
Was a sinner by Nature, and justly accurst;
And "Salvation by Grace" was the wonderful plan,
Which God had invented to save erring man.
'Twas the only atonement he knew how to make,
To annul the effects of his own sad mistake.

Now this was the doctrine of good Parson Brown,
Who preached, not long since, in a small country
 town.
He was zealous, and earnest, and could so excel
In describing the tortures of sinners in Hell,
That a famous revival commenced in the place,
And hundreds of souls found "Salvation by Grace;"
But he felt that he had not attained his desire,
Till he had converted one Peter McGuire.

This man was a blacksmith, frank, fearless and bold,
With great brawny sinews like Vulcan of old;
He had little respect for what ministers preach,
And sometimes was very profane in his speech.
His opinions were founded in clear common sense,
And he spoke as he thought, though he oft gave offense;
But however wanting, in whole or in part,
He was sound, and all right, when you came to his heart.

One day the good parson, with pious intent,
To the smithy of Peter most hopefully went;
And there, while the hammer industriously swung,
He preached, and he prayed, and exhorted, and sung,
And warned, and entreated poor Peter to fly
From the pit of destruction before he should die;
And to wash himself clean from the world's sinful strife,
In the Blood of the Lamb, and the River of Life.

Well, and what would you now be inclined to expect
Was the probable issue and likely effect?

Why, he swore "like a Pirate," and what do you
    think?
From a little black bottle took something to
    drink!
And he said, "I'll not mention the Blood of the
    Lamb,
But as for that River it aren't worth a —— ;"
Then pausing — as if to restrain his rude force —
He quietly added, "a mill-dam, of course."

Quick out of the smithy the minister fled,
As if a big bomb-shell had burst near his head;
And as he continued to haste on his way,
He was too much excited to sing or to pray;
But he thought how that some were elected by
    Grace,
As heirs of the kingdom — made sure of their
    place —
While others were doomed to the pains of Hell-
    fire,
And if e'er there was *one* such, 'twas Peter
    McGuire.

That night, when the Storm King was riding on
    high,
And the red shafts of lightning gleamed bright
    through the sky,

The church of the village, "the Temple of God,"
Was struck, for the want of a good lightning rod,
And swiftly descending, the element dire
Set the minister's house, close beside it, on fire,
While he peacefully slumbered, with never a fear
Of the terrible work of destruction so near.

There were Mary, and Hannah, and Tommy, and Joe,
All sweetly asleep in the bedroom below,
While their father was near, with their mother at rest,
(Like the wife of John Rogers with "one at the breast.")
But Alice, the eldest, a gentle young dove,
Was asleep all alone, in the room just above;
And when the wild cry of the rescuer came,
She only was left to the pitiless flame.

The fond mother counted her treasures of love,
When lo! one was missing — "O Father above!"
How madly she shrieked in her agony wild —
"My Alice! My Alice! O, save my dear child!"
Then down on his knees fell the Parson, and prayed
That the terrible wrath of the Lord might be stayed.

Said Peter McGuire, "Prayer is good in its place,
But then it don't suit *this* particular case."

He turned down the sleeves of his red flannel
  shirt,
To shield his great arms all besmutted with dirt;
Then into the billows of smoke and of fire,
Not pausing an instant, dashed Peter McGuire.
O, that terrible moment of anxious suspense!
How breathless their watching! their fear how
  intense!
And then their great joy! which was freely ex-
  pressed
When Peter appeared with the child on his breast.

A shout rent the air when the darling he laid
In the arms of her mother, so pale and dismayed;
And as Alice looked up and most gratefully
  smiled,
He bowed down his head and he wept like a
  child.
O, those tears of brave manhood that rained o'er
  his face,
Showed the true Grace of Nature, and the Nature
  of Grace;
'Twas a manifest token, a visible sign,
Of the indwelling life of the Spirit Divine.

Consider such natures, and then, if you can,
Preach of "total depravity" innate in man.
Talk of blasphemy! why, 'tis profanity wild!
To say that the Father thus cursed his own child.
Go learn of the stars, and the dew-spangled sod,
That all things rejoice in the *goodness* of God —
That each thing created is good *in its place*,
And Nature is but the *expression* of Grace.

HYMN OF THE ANGELS.

O Sacred Presence! Life Divine!
We rear for thee no gilded shrine—
Unfashioned by the hand of Art,
Thy temple is the child-like heart.
No tearful eye, no bended knee,
No servile speech we bring to Thee;
For thy great love tunes every voice,
And makes each trusting soul rejoice.
    Then strike your lyres,
    Ye angel choirs!
    The sound prolong,
    O white-robed throng!
Till every creature joins the song.

We will not mock Thy holy name
With titles high, of empty fame,
For Thou, with all Thy works and ways,
Art far beyond our feeble praise;
But freely as the birds that sing,
The soul's spontaneous gift we bring,

And like the fragrance of the flowers,
We consecrate to Thee our powers.
  Then strike your lyres,
   Ye angel choirs!
  The sound prolong,
   O white-robed throng!
 Till every creature joins the song.

All souls in circling orbits run,
Around Thee as their central sun;
And as the planets roll and burn,
To Thee, O Lord! for light we turn.
Nor Life, nor Death, nor Time, nor Space,
Shall rob us of our name or place,
But we shall love Thee, and adore
Through endless ages — Evermore!
  Then strike your lyres,
   Ye angel choirs!
  The sound prolong,
   O white-robed throng!
 Till every creature joins the song.

GONE HOME.

They called her, from the better land,
    And one bright spirit led the way;
She saw the angel's beckoning hand,
    And felt she could no longer stay.
O white-robed Peace! thy gentle cross
    Gave to her trusting heart no pain,
And that which is our earthly loss,
    Is unto her, eternal gain.

"God is a Spirit"—we can trust
    That she has left earth's shadows dim,
And laid aside her earthly dust,
    To grow in likeness unto Him.
"God is a Spirit"—"God is Love"—
    And closely folded to his breast,
Her spirit, like a tender dove,
    Shall in His love securely rest.

O, it was meet that flower-wreathed Spring,
    With forms of living beauty rife,
Should see the perfect blossoming
    Of this bright spirit into life.
The flowers will bloom upon her grave,
    The holy stars look down at night,
But where bright palms immortal wave,
    She will rejoice in cloudless light.

O, sweeter than the breath of flowers,
    Or dews that summer roses weep,
Deep in these loving hearts of ours
    Her blessèd memory we will keep.
Bright spirit, let thy light be given,
    With tender and celestial ray,
Beaming like some pure star from heaven,
    To guide us in our earthly way.

Clad in thine immortality,
    E'en now we hear thee joyful sing —
"O Grave, where is thy victory!
    O Death, where is thy sting!"
Pass on, sweet spirit, to increase
    In every bright, celestial grace,
Till in the land of love and peace,
    We meet thee, dear one, face to face.

THE CRY OF THE DESOLATE.

"It is only with Renunciation, that life, properly speaking, can be said to begin."

"Light dawns upon me! There is in man a HIGHER than love of *Happiness;* he can do without happiness, and instead thereof find *Blessedness.*" — THOS. CARLYLE.

O GOD of the Eagle and Lion!
    Thy strength to my being impart;
Not for wings, nor for sinews of iron,
    I ask, but thy life in my heart.
I grope in the dark, and seek blindly
    The hand that shall lead to the light;
There is no one to answer me kindly —
    There is no one to teach me the right.

An arrow from Fate's deadly quiver
    Seemed carelessly sped, at no mark,
But with anguish I tremble and shiver,
    For it wounded my soul in the dark.

I have suffered in silence unbroken,
    I have stanched the red wound with my hand;
O God! was the arrow Thy token?
    Did Fate but obey Thy command?

There is no one on earth that can render
    My heart its full measure of love;
There is no one on earth that is tender
    And true as the angels above.
Take me up to Thy bosom, O strong One!
    O wise One! I *am* not afraid!
For I know that Thou never wilt wrong one
    Of those whom Thy wisdom hath made.

These vestments of flesh that oppress us,
    Have stifled the soul's vital breath,
Like the torturing garment of Nessus,*
    We part from them only in death.
O Thou marvelous Soul of Existence!
    Are we doomed by the might of Thy will,
Unchanged by our feeble resistance,
    Thy fathomless law to fulfill?

O Fashioner! Thou who hast guided
    The tempest of atoms at strife,
Hath not Thy compassion provided
    A fountain of strength for each life?

---

* The garment which caused the death of Hercules.

And doth not Time's changing phantasma
   Still move at Thy sovereign control,
As when in Earth's cherishing plasma
   Was planted the germ of the soul?

Then lead me, for O, I am lonely!
   And love me, for I am Thine own —
Yes, Great One and True One! Thine only —
   And with Thee am never alone.
O God of the Eagle and Lion!
   Thy strength to my being impart;
Not for wings, nor for sinews of iron
   I ask — but Thy life in my heart.

THE SPIRIT-MOTHER.

Through our lives' mysterious changes,
  Through the sorrow-haunted years,
Runs a law of Compensation
  For our sufferings and our tears.
And the soul that reasons rightly,
  All its sad complaining stills,
Till it learns that meek submission,
  Where it wishes not nor wills.

Thus, in Sorrow's fiery furnace
  Was a faithful mother tried,
Till, through Love's divinest uses,
  All her soul was purified.
O ye sorrow-stricken mothers!
  Ye whose weakness feeds your pain!
Listen to her simple story —
  Listen! and be strong again.

"It was sunset — and the day-dream
  Of my life was almost o'er;
For my spirit-bark was drifting
  Slowly, slowly from the shore.

Dimly could I see the sunlight
  Through my vine-wreathed window shine,
Faintly could I feel the pressure
  Of a strong hand clasping mine.

"But anew the life-tide started,
  At my infant's feeble cry;
Back my spirit turned in anguish,
  And I felt I could not die.
Deeper, darker fell the shadows,
  Like the midnight's sable pall,
And that infant cry grew fainter —
  Fainter — fainter — that was all!

"Suddenly I heard sweet voices
  Mingling in a tender strain —
All my mortal weakness left me,
  All my anguish and my pain.
On my forehead fell the glory
  Of the bright, celestial morn,
I was of the earth no longer,
  For my spirit was re-born.

"Pure, sweet faces bent above me,
  Tenderly they gazed and smiled,
And my Angel-Mother whispered,
  'Welcome, welcome home, my child!'

Then, in one melodious chorus,
   Sang the radiant angel band,
'Welcome! O thou weary pilgrim!
   Welcome to the Spirit Land!'

"But, o'er all those glad rejoicings,
   Rose again my infant's cry,
For my heart had borne the echo
   Through the portals of the sky.
And I murmured, O ye bright ones!
   Still my earthly home is dear;
Vain are all your songs of welcome,
   For I am not happy here.

"Strike your harps, ye white-robed Angels!
   But your music makes me wild,
For my heart is with my treasure,
   Heaven is only with my child!
Let me go, and whisper comfort
   To my little mourning dove —
Life is cold; O, let me shield him
   With a mother's tenderest love!

"Swift there came a pure, white angel,
   Through the glory, shining far,
In her hand she bore a lily,
   On her forehead beamed a star.

Very beautiful and tender
    Was the love-light in her eyes,
Like the sunny smile of Summer,
    Beaming in the azure skies.

"And she said, 'O, mourning sister!
    Lo! thy prayer of love is heard,
For the boundless Heart of Being
    By thine earnest cry is stirred.
Heaven is life's divinest freedom,
    And no mandate bids thee stay;
Go, and as a star of duty,
    Guide thy loved one on his way.

"'Life is full of holy uses,
    If but rightly understood,
And its evils and abuses
    May be stepping-stones to good.
Never seek to weakly shield him,
    Or his destiny control,
For the wealth that grief shall yield him,
    Is the birthright of his soul.'

"Musing deeply on her meaning,
    Turned I from the heavenly shore,
And on love's swift wings descending,
    Sought my earthly home once more.

There my widowed, childless sister
    Sat with meek and quiet grace,
With her heart's great, wasting sorrow,
    Written on her pale, sweet face.

"And she sang in dreamy murmurs,
    Bending o'er my Willie's head,
'Hush, my dear, lie still and slumber,
    Holy angels guard thy bed.'
Soft I whispered, 'Dearest sister —
    Darling Willie — I am here.'
Sweetly smiled the sleeping infant,
    And the singer dropped a tear.

"Thenceforth was my soul united
    To that life more dear than mine;
And I prayed for strength to guide me,
    From the source of Life Divine.
Slowly did I see the meaning
    In life's purposes concealed —
All the uses of temptation,
    Sin and sorrow, stood revealed.

"Through my loved one's youth and manhood,
    In the hour of sinful strife,
I could see the nobler issues,
    And the grand design of life.

I could see that he was guided
  By a mightier hand than mine,
And a mother's love was weakness,
  By the side of Love Divine.

"Then I did not seek to shield him,
  Or his destiny control —
Life, with all its varied changes,
  Was the teacher of his soul.
Nay, I did not strive to alter
  What I could not make nor mend,
For the love so full of wisdom,
  Could be trusted to the end.

"I could give him strength and courage,
  From the treasures of my love —
I could lead his aspirations
  To the holy heart above;
I could warn him in temptation,
  That he might not blindly fall;
I could wait with faith and patience
  For his triumph — that was all.

"'Mid the rush and roar of battle,
  In the carnival of death,
When the air grew hot and heavy,
  With the cannon's fiery breath,

First and foremost with the bravest,
   Who had heard their country's call,
With the stars and stripes above him,
   Did my darling Willie fall.

"Onward — onward rushed his comrades,
   With a wild, defiant cry,
As they charged upon the foeman,
   Leaving him alone to die.
Faint he murmured, 'O, my mother!
   Angel mother! art thou near?'
And he caught the whispered answer,
   'Darling Willie, I am here!

"'O, my loved one! my true-hearted!
   Soon your anguish will be o'er;
Then, in heaven's eternal sunshine,
   We shall dwell for evermore.'
Swiftly o'er his pallid features,
   Gleams of heavenly brightness passed,
And my Willie's noble spirit
   Met me face to face at last.

"In a soldier's grave they laid him,
   Underneath the sheltering pines,
Where the breezes made sweet music,
   Through the gently swaying vines.

Now in heaven, our souls united,
    All their aspirations blend,
And my spirit's holy mission
    Thus hath found a joyful end."

Through our lives' mysterious changes,
    Through the sorrow-haunted years,
Runs a law of Compensation
    For our sufferings and our tears;
And the soul that reasons rightly,
    All its sad complaining stills,
Till it gains that calm condition,
    Where it wishes not, nor wills.

FACE THE SUNSHINE.

O, a morbid fancy had David Bell,
That over his path like a wizard spell,
A great, black shadow forever fell.
He turned his back on the sun's clear ray;
From a singing bird, or a child at play,
With a nervous shudder he shrank away;
  And he shook his head,
  As he gloomily said,
"This shadow will haunt me till I am dead!"

In the solemn shade of the forest wide,
Or in the churchyard at eventide,
Like a gloomy ghost he was seen to glide.
There, nursing his fancies all alone,
He would sit him down with a dismal moan,
In the dewy grass by some moss-grown stone,
  And shake his head,
  As he gloomily said,
"This shadow will haunt me till I am dead!"

Never a nod or a smile would greet
Old David Bell, in the field or street,
From the sturdy yeoman he chanced to meet.
The children fled from his path away,
And the good wives whispered, "Alack a day!
The Devil hath led his soul astray!"
   For he ever said,
   As he shook his head,
"This shadow will haunt me till I am dead!"

One Sabbath morn when the air was balm,
And the green earth smiled with a heavenly
   charm,
In the peaceful hush, in the holy calm,
Old David Bell, with a new intent,
Across the bridge o'er the mill-stream went,
And his steps towards the village chapel bent.
   For he said, "I will try
   From this fiend to fly,
And escape the shadow before I die!"

But all along on the sandy road,
His great, gaunt shadow before him strode,
Like a fiend escaped from its dark abode.
Sometimes it crouched in an angle small,
Then up it leapt, like a giant tall;
And as David noticed these changes all,

He shook his head,
As he gloomily said,
"This shadow will haunt me till I am dead!"

At length, he came to the chapel door,
But the great, gaunt shadow went in before,
Leaping and dancing along the floor.
Old David mournfully turned away —
He could not enter to praise and pray,
While that impish shadow before him lay.
And he shook his head,
As he gloomily said,
"This shadow will haunt me till I am dead!"

He wandered away, not heeding where,
To a lonely grave, where a willow fair
Whispered sweet words to the summer air.
But he saw not the long, lithe branches wave,
For only a weary look he gave
At his own black shadow, across the grave.
And he shook his head,
As he gloomily said,
"This shadow will haunt me till I am dead!"

"Nay, nay, good David!" a voice replied.
He turned him quickly, and close by his side
Stood old Goody Gay, known far and wide.

Though Time had stolen her bloom away,
And changed the gold of her locks to gray,
Her face was bright as the summer day.
  "Don't shake your head!"
  She cheerfully said,
"But face the sunshine, good man, instead!"

With a hopeless look, and a sigh profound,
He sat himself down by the grassy mound,
Where the bright-eyed daisies grew thick around.
"Nay, leave me," he said, in a sullen tone,
"For I and the shadow would be alone;
No balm of healing for me is known.
  It will be as I said,
  This thing that I dread,
This shadow, will haunt me till I am dead."

The good dame answered, "O, David Bell!
Why will ye be ringing your own heart's knell?
For I tell ye this, that I know full well—
The blessèd Father, who loves us all,
Who notices even a sparrow's fall,
Is never deaf to His children's call;
  His love is our light
  In the darkest night:
Just turn to *that* sunshine, and all is right."

"In this very grave did I lay to rest,
With his pale hands folded upon his breast,
The one of all others I loved the best.
And then, though my heart in its anguish yearned,
My face to the sunshine I ever turned,
And thus a great lesson of life I learned;
  Which you, too, will find,
  If you will but mind,
That thus, all life's shadows are cast behind."

He gazed in her earnest face as she spoke,
And then a light o'er his features broke,
As if new life in his soul awoke.
There was something so bright in that summer
  day,
And the cheerful language of Goody Gay,
That his morbid fancies were charmed away;
  And he said, "I will try,
  For it may be, that I
Shall escape this shadow before I die."

He turned him around on the grassy knoll,
And flush o'er his forehead and into his soul
The warmth of the gladdening sunshine stole.
The good dame lifted a willow bough,
And gently laid her hand on his brow —
"Say, David, where is your shadow now?

>   The shadow has fled,
>   But ye are not dead.
> Look up to the sunshine, man! Hold up your
>   head!"

Still athwart the grave did the shadow lay,
But the face of David was turned away,
And lifted up to the sun's clear ray.
Then the light of truth on his spirit fell,
Breaking forever the magic spell
That darkened the vision of David Bell.
  His trial was past;
  And the shadow, at last,
Behind him there, on the grave was cast.

O, ye! who toil o'er your earthly way,
With your faces turned from the truth's clear ray,
Consider the counsel of Goody Gay.
Though shadows should haunt you as black as
  night,
Be faithful and firm to your highest light,
And face the sunshine with all of your might!
  Keep a cheerful mind,
  And at length you will find
That the grave, and life's shadows, all lie behind.

HESTER VAUGHN.

[Hester Vaughn was tried for the crime of infanticide. She was convicted, and sentence of death passed upon her. Subsequently, by the efforts of benevolent individuals, and the pressure of public opinion, her sentence was commuted to imprisonment for life. Susan A. Smith, M. D., of Philadelphia, who visited her in prison, and was chiefly instrumental in obtaining her reprieve, gives the following statement in relation to the circumstances attendant upon her alleged crime: "She was deserted by her husband, who knew she had not a relative in America. She rented a third-story room in this city (Philadelphia), from a German family, who understood very little English. She furnished this room, found herself in food and fuel for three months on twenty dollars. She was taken sick in this room at midnight, on the 6th of February, and lingered until Saturday morning, the 8th, when her child was born. She told me she was nearly frozen, and fainted or went to sleep for a long time. Through all this period of *agony* she was *alone*, without *nourishment* or *fire*, with her door unfastened. It has been asserted that she confessed her guilt. I can solemnly say in the presence of Almighty God that she never confessed guilt to me, and stoutly affirms that no such word ever passed her lips."]

Now by the common weal and woe,
 Uniting each with all;
And by the snares we may not know,
 Until we blindly fall —
Let every heart by sorrow tried,
 Let every *woman* born,
Feel that her cause stands side by side
 With that of Hester Vaughn.

A woman, famished for the love
    All hearts so deeply crave,
Whose only hope was Heaven above,
    To succor and to save;
With only want, and woe, and care,
    To greet her child unborn;
A weary burden, hard to bear,
    Was life to Hester Vaughn.

No friend, no food, no fire, no light,
    And face to face with death,
She struggled through the weary night,
    With anguish in each breath;
Till that frail life which shared her own,
    Had perished ere the morn,
And left her to the hearts of stone,
    That judged poor Hester Vaughn.

Who was it, that refused to draw
    A lesson from the time,
And in the name of human law,
    Pronounced her grief a crime?
Was her accuser, cold and stern,
    A man of woman born,
Whose *debt* to woman could not earn
    Some grace for Hester Vaughn?

The word of judgment is not sure,
    To wealth and station high,
But that she was *alone* and *poor*,
    Was she condemned to die.
O God of justice! for whose grace
    The servile worldlings fawn,
Has not thy love a hiding-place
    For such as Hester Vaughn?

Come to the bar of Judgment, come,
    Ye favored ones of earth,
And let your haughty lips be dumb,
    So boastful of your worth.
What virtues, or what noble deeds,
    Your faithless lives adorn,
That thus by laws, or lifeless creeds,
    You sentence Hester Vaughn?

What countless crimes, what guilt untold,
    What depths of sin and shame,
Are gilded by your lying gold,
    Or hidden by a name!
Ye pave your social hells with skulls
    Of Infants yet unborn;
Then virtuous wrath suspicion lulls,
    And crushes Hester Vaughn.

Ye, who your secret sins confess,
    Before the Eternal Throne —
Adulterer and Adulteress!
    What mercy have *ye* shown?
For place and power, for gems and gold,
    Ye give your souls in pawn,
But Heaven's fair gates will first unfold
    To such as Hester Vaughn.

The "mills of God that grind so slow,"
    Will "grind exceeding small;"
And time, at length, will clearly show
    The want or worth of all.
Distinctions will not always be
    With such precision drawn,
Between the proud of high degree
    And such as Hester Vaughn.

Through Moyamensing's prison bars,[*]
    She counts each weary day,
Or 'neath the calmly watching stars,
    She wakes to weep and pray.
Thank God! for her in heaven above,
    A brighter day will dawn,
And those who judge all hearts in love,
    Will welcome Hester Vaughn.

---

[*] Since the above poem was given, through the pressure of public opinion, she has been pardoned, and sent back to England.

SONG OF THE SPIRIT CHILDREN.

LET us sing the praise of Love —
Holy Spirit! Heavenly Dove!
Bringing on its blessèd wings
Life to all created things.
Wheresoe'er its light is shed,
Sorrow lifts its drooping head,
And the tears of grief that start
Turn to sunshine in the heart.
      Love divine,
        All things are thine!
Every creature seeks thy shrine.
And thy boundless blessings fall
With an equal love on all.

Let us sing the praise of Love,
Everywhere — around, above;
Watching with its starry eyes,
From the blue of boundless skies,
Heeding when the lowly call,
Mindful of a sparrow's fall,

Writing on the flower-wreathed sod,
"God is love, and love is God."
  Love divine,
   All things are thine!
 Every creature seeks thy shrine!
 And thy boundless blessings fall
 With an equal love on all.

Let us sing the praise of Love —
Fairest of all things above.
How its blesséd sunshine lies
In the light of loving eyes!
And when words are all too weak,
How its deeds of mercy speak!
They who learn to love aright,
Pass from darkness into light.
  Love divine,
   All things are thine!
 Every creature seeks thy shrine!
 And thy boundless blessings fall
 With an equal love on all.

Let us sing the praise of Love —
Shepherd of the lambs above,
Nothing can forbid, that we
Come in trusting love to Thee.

Fold us closely to Thy heart,
Make us of Thyself a part;
All the heaven our souls have known,
We have found in Thee alone.
   Love divine,
    All things are thine!
  Every creature seeks thy shrine!
  And thy boundless blessings fall
  With an equal love on all.

HE GIVETH HIS BELOVED SLEEP.

Night drops her mantle from the skies,
   And from her home of peace above,
She watches with her starry eyes,
   As with a tender mother's love.
The sounds of toil and strife are stilled,
   And in the silence calm and deep,
The word of promise is fulfilled —
   "He giveth his belovéd sleep."

The weary soul oppressed with care,
   The young, the old, the strong, the weak,
The rich, the poor, the brave, the fair,
   Alike the common blessing seek.
The child sleeps on its mother's breast,
   The broken-hearted cease to weep,
For answering to the prayer for rest,
   "He giveth his belovéd sleep."

Beneath the churchyard's sod there lies
    Full many a weary form at rest,
With death's calm slumber in the eyes,
    And pale hands folded on the breast.
O ye who bend above the sod,
    And tears of silent anguish weep,
Lean with a firmer faith on God —
    "He giveth his belovéd sleep," —

Sleep for the eye whose light has fled,
    Sleep for the weary heart and hand;
But not the sleep of those who tread
    The green hills of "the better land."
No restless nights of pain are theirs,
    No weary watch for morn they keep,
But through release from mortal cares,
    "He giveth his belovéd sleep."

Theirs is that sweet, exceeding peace,
    Where love makes every duty blest,
Where anxious cares and longings cease,
    And labor in itself is rest.
O, we will trust the power above
    The treasures of our hearts to keep,
Safe folded in his arms of love,
    "He giveth *our* belovéd sleep."

THE FAMISHED HEART.

The following poem was given at the conclusion of a lecture upon "Jesus the Medium, and Socrates the Philosopher."

"A new commandment I give unto you, that ye love one another."
                                        JOHN xiii. 34.

O YE! upon whose favored shrine
   Love hath a rich libation poured —
Who, even as a thing divine,
   Are fondly worshiped and adored —
Spare but one kindly thought for those
   Who stand in loneliness apart,
Worn by that weariest of woes,
   The hopeless hunger of the heart.

As deadly as the dagger's thrust,
   Envenomed as a serpent's fangs,
It eats like slow, corroding rust,
   And lengthens out in lingering pangs.

Think not with careless jest or smile
    To pass this wasting sorrow by;
For countless hearts attest the while,
    That thus, alas! too many die.

I once was of the earth like you;
    I loved, and hoped, and feared as well,
But on my heart the kindly dew
    Of fond affection never fell.
An orphan in my early years,
    Mine was a hard and cheerless lot,
For I was doomed, with prayers and tears,
    To seek for love and find it not.

A bird upon a stormy sea,
    A lamb without a sheltering fold,
A vine with no supporting tree,
    A blossom blighted by the cold, —
The warmth of kindly atmospheres
    Gave to my life no quickened start;
Love's sunshine melted not to tears
    The drifted sorrows of my heart.

Fresh from the innocence of youth,
    I entered on the rude world's strife,
But evermore this venomed tooth
    Was gnawing at the root of life.

O, I was but a thing of dust!
   And what should save me from my fall?
The tempter whispered, "Lawless lust
   Is better than no love at all!"

Then with a flinty face I turned,
   Defiant of the social ban,
For my poor, famished nature yearned
   For e'en such sympathy from man.
But no! I heard, as from above,
   This truth that many learn too late,
That man's unhallowed, selfish love,
   Is far more cruel than his hate.

I shrank from Passion's burning breath,
   Those sensuous lips and eyes of flame,
And from that furnace fire of death
   My outraged heart unblemished came.
But darker, deeper grew the night
   That closed around my suffering soul,
And Fate's black billows, flecked with white,
   O'er all my being seemed to roll.

At length, within a maniac's cell,
   I moaned and muttered day by day,
Till, like a loathsome thing, I fell
   From human consciousness away.

That nightmare dream of life was brief,
  For horror choked my struggling breath,
And my poor heart, with love and grief,
  Was famished even unto death.

Unconscious of my spirit's change,
  Long did I linger near the earth,
Until a being, kind, though strange,
  Recalled me to my conscious worth.
From thence I seemed to be transformed,
  Renewed as by redeeming grace,
And then my soul the purpose formed —
  To seek "the Saviour of the race."

My aspirations served to bear
  My earnest spirit swift away,
Until a heaven, serene and fair,
  My onward progress seemed to stay.
I came where two immortals trod,
  In friendly converse, side by side;
"O, lead me to the Son of God,
  That I may worship him!" I cried.

One turned — and from his aspect mild
  A benison of love was shed —
"O, say, whom do you seek, dear child?
  We all are sons of God," he said.

"Nay, nay!" I cried, "not such I mean!
  But him who died on Calvary—
The humble-hearted Nazarene!"
  He meekly answered, "*I am he!*"

"O, then, as sinful Mary knelt,
  In tearful sorrow, at thy feet,
So does my icy nature melt,
  And her sweet reverence I repeat.
O God! O Christ! O Living All!
  'Thou art the Life, the Truth, the Way';
Lo! at thy feet I humbly fall—
  Cast not my sinful soul away!"

"Poor bleeding heart! poor wounded dove!"
  In tones of gentleness, he said:
"How hast thou famished for that love
  Which is indeed 'the living bread.'
Kneel not to me; the Power Divine,
  Than I, is greater, mightier far;
His glories lesser lights outshine,
  As noonday hides the brightest star."

"You died for all the world!" I cried,
  "And therefore do I bend the knee."
"My friend,"* he answered, "at my side,
  Long ere I suffered, died for me.

    * Socrates.

He drained for man the poisoned cup,
　I gave my body to the cross,
But when the sum is counted up,
　Great is our gain, and small our loss.

"Not thus would I be deified,
　Or claim the homage that men pay;
But he who takes me for his guide,
　Makes me his Life, his Truth, his Way.
O, heaven shall not descend to man,
　Nor man ascend to heaven above,
Till he shall see Salvation's plan
　Is written in the law of love.

"Dear sister! let your fears depart —
　I have no power to bid you live,
But I can feed your famished heart
　Upon the love I freely give.
Mine are the hearts that men condemn,
　Or crush in their ambitious strife,
And through my love I am to them
　'The Resurrection and the Life.'"

He raised me gently from his feet,
　And laid my head upon his breast.
O God! how calm, how pure and sweet,
　How more than peaceful was that rest!

I feel that blessèd presence yet—
It fills me with a joy serene—
Nor have I hungered since I met
The gentle-hearted Nazarene.

THE TRIUMPH OF LIFE.

The following poem, given under the inspiration of Mrs. Hemans, is a reversion of the ideas contained in a poem composed by her in earth life, entitled " The Hour of Death."

" Leaves have their time to fall,
　And flowers to wither at the north wind's breath,
　And stars to set — but all,
　　Thou hast all seasons for thine own, O Death!"

LEAVES have their glad recall,
　And blossoms open to the South wind's breath,
And stars that set shall rise again, for all,
　All things shall triumph o'er the Spoiler — Death.

Day was not made for care —
　Eve brings bright angels to the joyous hearth —
Night comes with dreams of peace, and visions fair
　Of those whom Death could conquer not on earth.

When, in the festive hour,
   Death mingles poison with the ruby wine,
Life also comes with overwhelming power,
   Changing the deadly draught to life divine.

Youth and the opening rose
   May vanish from the outward sight away,
But Life their inward beauty shall disclose,
   And rob the haughty Spoiler of his prey.

Leaves have their glad recall,
   And blossoms open to the South wind's breath,
And stars that set shall rise again, for all,
   All things shall triumph o'er the Spoiler — Death.

We know that yet again
   Our loved and lost shall cross the Summer sea,
Bearing with them the sheaves of golden grain,
   Which they have harvested, O Life! with thee.

Thy breath is in the gale
   Whose kiss unseals the violet's azure eye;
And though the roses in our path grow pale,
   We know that all things change, they do not die.

Wherever man may roam,
  Thy presence, viewless as the Summer air,
Meets him abroad, or in his peaceful home,
  And when Death calls him forth, thou, too, art there.

Thou art where soul meets soul,
  Or where earth's noblest fall in battle strife;
But Death, the Spoiler, yields to thy control;
  Forevermore thou art the conqueror, Life.

Leaves have their glad recall,
  And blossoms open to the South wind's breath,
And stars that set shall rise again, for all,
  All things shall triumph o'er the Spoiler — Death.

REFORMERS.

Where have the world's great heroes gone,
    The champions of the Right,
Who, with their armor girded on,
    Have passed beyond our sight?
Are they where palms immortal wave,
    And laurels crown the brow?
Or was the victory thine, O Grave?
    Where are they? Answer thou.

We shudder at the silence dread,
    That renders no·reply —
O, dust! from whence the soul hath fled,
    Thou canst not hear our cry.
The violet, o'er their mouldering clay,
    Looks meekly from the sod,
But tells not of the hidden way
    Their angel feet have trod.

Where are they, Death? thou mighty one!
    To some far land unknown,
Beyond the stars, beyond the sun,
    Have their bright spirits flown?

Their hearts were strong through Truth and Right,
  Life's stormy tide to stem.
O Death! thou conqueror of might!
  What need hadst thou of them?

The earth is green with martyrs' graves,
  On hill, and plain, and shore,
And the great ocean's sounding waves
  Sweep over thousands more.
For us they drained life's bitter cup,
  And dared the battle strife;
Where are they, Death? O, render up
  The secret of their life!

We listen — to our earnest cries
  No answer is made known,
Save the "Resurgam" — I *shall* rise!
  Carved on the burial stone.
O Grave! O Death! thou canst not keep
  The spark of Life Divine;
They have no need of rest or sleep;
  Nay, Death, they are not thine!

Where are they? O Creative Soul!
  To whom no name is given,
Whose presence fills the boundless whole,
  Whose love alone is heaven,

Through all the long, eternal hours
  What toils do they pursue?
Are their great souls still linked with ours,
  To suffer and to do?

Lo! how the viewless air around
  With quickening life is stirred,
And from the silences profound
  Leaps forth the answering word,
"We live — not in some distant sphere
  Life's mission to fulfill;
But, joined with faithful spirits here,
  We love and labor still.

No laurel wreath, no waving palm,
  No royal robes are ours,
But evermore, serene and calm,
  We use life's noblest powers.
Toil on in hope, and bravely bear
  The burdens of your lot;
Great, earnest souls your labors share;
  They will forsake you not."

MR. DE SPLAE.

It may seem a strange question, good people, but say,
Did you never hear tell of one Mr. De Splae?
A man who made up for the lack of good sense
By a wondrous amount of mere show and pretense;
Puffed up with conceit like an airy balloon,
He was hard to approach as the "man in the moon,"
Save when for some *purpose* it came in his way,
And then, O how gracious was Mr. De Splae!

A sly politician, a popular man,
When all things went smoothly he marshaled the van;
But when there was aught like a failure to fear,
He quickly deserted or fell to the rear.
His speech for the people went "gayly and glib,"
While he drew his support from the National crib;

But when an assessment or tax was to pay,
O, how outraged and angry was Mr. De Splae!

He smoked, and he chewed, and he drank, and he
    swore;
But then every man whom the ladies adore,
Is prone to these failings — some more and some
    less,
Which are all overlooked in a man of address.
It also was whispered that he had betrayed
The too trusting faith of an innocent maid;
But the ladies all blamed *her* for going astray,
While they pardoned and petted — " dear Mr.
    De Splae."

There was good Mr. Honest, who lived but next
    door,
He was true, and substantial, and sound to the
    core;
He had made it the rule of his life, from his
    youth,
To shun all evasions and speak the plain truth;
But *the ladies* — who always are judges, you know,
Declared him to be a detestable beau —.
Not worthy of mention within the same day,
With that *pink of perfection* — " dear Mr. De
    Splae."

Withal he was pious — perhaps you will smile,
And ask how he happened the church to beguile;
Why, the churches accept men for better or worse,
If there's only a plenty of cash in the purse.
Gold still buys remission as freely and fast,
As it did in the Catholic Church in the past.
'Tis the same thing right over, and that was the way,
That the church swallowed smoothly "*good* Mr. De Splae."

O, you ought to have heard him when leading in prayer!
How he flattered the Father of All for his care,
And confessed he was sinful a thousand times o'er,
Which 'twas morally certain the Lord knew before.
The ladies responded in sweet little sighs,
With their elegant handkerchiefs pressed to their eyes,
But the pure, unseen spirits turned sadly away
From the loud-mouthed devotions of Mr. De Splae.

O, short-sighted mortal! Poor Mr. De Splae!
His mask of deception was molded in clay,

And when his external in death was let fall,
What he was, without seeming, was known unto
    all.
His garment of patches — his flimsy disguise —
Which had won him distinction in other men's
    eyes,
Was "changed in a twinkling" — ay, vanished
    away,
Leaving nothing to boast of to Mr. De Splae.

Ah, a great reputation, a title, or name,
Oft brings its possessor to sorrow and shame;
But a *character*, founded in goodness and worth,
Outlasts all the perishing glories of earth.
O'er the frailties of nature, and changes of time,
It rises majestic, in beauty sublime,
Till the weak and faint-hearted are cheered by its
    ray,
Far above all mere seeming and empty display.

WILL IT PAY?

    Men may say what they will
    Of the Author of Ill,
And the wiles of the Devil that tempt them astray,
    But there's something far worse —
    A more terrible curse —
It is selling the Truth for the sake of the pay.

    Like Judas of old,
    For silver or gold,
Man often has bartered his conscience away,
    Has walked in disguise,
    And has trafficked in lies,
If the prospect was good that the business would pay.

    If a fortune is made
    By cheating in trade,
It is seldom, if ever, men question the way;
    But they make it a rule
    That a man is a fool
Who strives to make justice and honesty pay.

An instance more clear
Could never appear,
Than was seen in the life of old Nicholas Gray,
Who ne'er made a move,
In religion or love,
Unless he was sure that the venture would pay.

He built him a house
That would scarce hold a mouse,
Where he managed to live in a miserly way,
Till he said, "On my life,
I will take me a wife;
It is running a risk — but I think it will pay."

Then he opened a store,
Whose fair, tempting door,
Led sure and direct to destruction's broad way.
For liquor he sold,
To the young and the old,
To the poor and the wretched, and all who could pay.

A woman once came,
And in God's holy name,
She prayed him his terrible traffic to stay,
That her husband might not
Be a poor drunken sot,
And spend all his wages for what would not pay.

Old Nicholas laughed,
As his whisky he quaffed,
And he said, "If your husband comes hither to-day,
I will sell him his dram,
And I don't care a — clam
How *you* are supported if *I* get my pay."

So he prospered in sin,
And continued to win
The wages of death in this terrible way,
Till a Constable's raid
Put an end to his trade,
And closed up his business as well as the pay.

To church he then went,
With a pious intent
Of "getting religion" — as some people say —
For he said, "It comes cheap,
And costs nothing to keep,
And from close observation I think it will pay."

But the tax and the tithe
Made old Nicholas writhe,
And he thought that "the plate" came too often
his way;
So he soon fell from grace,
And made vacant his place,
For he said, "I perceive that religion don't pay."

Still striving to thrive,
And thriving to strive,
His attention was turned a political way;
But he could not decide
Which party or side
Would be the most likely to prosper or pay.

He was puzzled, and hence
He sat on the fence,
Prepared in an instant to jump either way;
But it fell to his fate
To jump just too late,
And he said in disgust, "This of *all* things don't pay."

Year passed after year,
And there did not appear
A spark of improvement in Nicholas Gray,
For his morals grew worse
With the weight of his purse,
As he managed to make his rascality pay.

At length he fell ill;
So he drew up his will,
Just in time to depart from his mansion of clay,
And he said to old Death,
With his last gasp of breath,
"Don't hunt for my soul, for I know it won't pay."

O, 'tis sad to rehearse,
In prose or in verse,
The faults and the follies that lead men astray.
For gold is but dross,
And a terrible loss,
When conscience and manhood are given in pay.

Then be not deceived,
Though men have believed
That 'tis lawful to sin in a general way,
But stick to the right
With all of your might,
For Truth is eternal, and always will pay.

THE LIVING WORD.

"In the beginning was the Word, and the Word was with God, and the Word was God."
"And the Word was made flesh and dwelt in men."

ETERNAL, Self-existent Soul!
   From whom Life's issues take their start,
Thou art the undivided Whole,
   Of whom each creature forms a part.
Thy boundless being's distant reach,
   Our finite vision may not see,
But this we know, that each with each,
   We live and move alone in Thee.

"In the beginning was the Word"—
   The Word, as present now, as then,
Which, in the heart of Nature, stirred
   "The Life which was the light of men."
Through Chaos and Confusion's night
   Streamed forth the light of Love divine,
And lit along Creation's hight,
   Unnumbered fires in glittering line.

Earth's fiery heart, with battle shocks,
   Beat fiercely in her granite breast,
Leaving on scarred and blackened rocks
   The record of her wild unrest.
Rich ores in molten currents swept —
   Like fire within her veins they ran —
While in the womb of Nature slept
   The embryo prophecy of man.

Down deep, the elements, like gnomes,
   Beside their flaming forges wrought,
To fashion shapes, and future homes
   For the embodiment of Thought.
The wild winds roared — the raging floods
   Tossed their defiant waves on high,
While from the old, primeval woods,
   The chorus thundered to the sky.

The broadcast, wondrous Encrinites
   Opened their breathing lily bells,
While Ammonites and Trilobites
   Paved pathless spaces with their shells.
The coral Polyp, 'neath the wave,
   Wrought in the great progressive plan,
By which the lesser creature's grave
   Built up the future home of man.

The slumbering Iguanodon*
   Lay reeking in mephitic damp —
The Mylodon and Mastodon
   Startled the forests with their tramp.
Gigantic ferns, like feathery palms,
   Nodded in silence to the trees,
Whose royal crests and stalwart arms
   Tossed like the waves of stormy seas.

Thus on, still on the current rolled —
   The light of countless mornings shone;
And radiant sunsets robed in gold,
   Swept down the gulfs of years unknown.
At length, with beasts, and birds, and flowers,
   Creation seemed a perfect whole;
Then God and Nature joined their powers,
   And man became a living soul.

O Mother Nature! Father God!
   How wondrous is the work we trace!
Man fashioned from the senseless clod,
   Yet filled with life's divinest grace.
Nor is that form of earthly mold
   The limit of his life to be;
Forth from the mortal will unfold
   The germ of immortality.

---

* Pronounced Ig-war-no-don.

For even as through countless throes,
  And travail pains, the mighty plan
Of God in Nature slowly rose,
  To consummate its aims in man,
Thus onward still the current rolls,
  The spirit with the flesh at strife,
Until, at length, all living souls
  Are quickened from the inmost life.

Across the broad, unfathomed sea,
  That breaks upon the shores of time,
The promise of the *yet to be*
  Comes like a prophecy sublime.
The purple gloom, that like a veil
  Rests on that ever swelling tide,
Full oft reveals a friendly sail,
  With tidings from the further side.

O soul of man! to conscious power
  From elements of death outwrought,
The Living Word forecast thine hour,
  And found the dwelling-place it sought.
High in the heavens forevermore,
  The stars of truth eternal shine;
Sail on, O man, from shore to shore;
  The power that guides thee is divine.

In the beginning was the Word —
　　The Word as present now as then —
And by its quickening power is stirred
　　New life within the souls of men.
Thus on, still on, the current rolls,
　　Through daisies blooming on the sod,
Through creeping things, though living souls,
　　Through "quickened spirits" up to God.

HYMN TO THE SUN.

O FOUNTAIN of beauty, of gladness and light,
Whose pathway is set in the infinite hight,
Whose light hath no shadow, whose day hath no
 night!

We know not thy birthplace, O wonderful one!
We count not the ages through which thou hast
 run,
But we render thee praises, O life-giving Sun.

All day the glad Earth in thy loving embrace,
Arrayed by thy bounty in garments of grace,
Lifts up to thy glances her beautiful face.

And at night, when her children need silence and
 rest,
With the light of her starry-eyed sisterhood
 blest,
She sleeps like a bride on thy cherishing breast.

When the skylark springs up at the coming of morn,
When the golden fringed curtains of night are withdrawn,
Then blushing with beauty the day is new born.

And the pulses of Nature in harmony bound,
To the waves of thy glory which move without sound,
And sweep unimpeded through spaces profound.

Ay, the life-tide that leaps in the bird or the flower —
The rainbow that gleams through the drops of the shower —
O wonderful artist! are born of thy power.

And the rush of the whirlwind, the roar of the deep,
The cataract's thunder, the avalanche-sweep,
Are thy forces majestic, aroused from their sleep.

Shall we wonder, that filled with devotion untold,
The awe-stricken Parsee adored thee of old,
Nor dreamed that One greater thy glory controlled?

And He, the Eternal, the Ancient of Days —
Whose splendors are veiled by inscrutable ways —
Did he frown on such blindness, or envy thee
     praise?

O Sun! in the light of whose presence we see,
We ask, — canst thou tell us? — what caused us
     to be?
And how are we linked to creation and thee?

We must perish — but thou, by thy wonderful
     powers,
Wilt rescue from darkness these bodies of ours,
And fashion them over to verdure and flowers.

But the jewel of beauty in life's golden bowl —
O, answer us — say — dost thou also control
That Infinite Essence, the life of the soul?

There is doubt, there is darkness and fear in our cry:
Dost thou drink up the pearl of our lives when
     we die?
We listen — but silence alone makes reply.

It is well — for our spirits may know by the sign,
That a might hath evoked thee far greater than
     thine,
And we must seek Truth at life's innermost shrine.

That Centre of Being, transcending all thought,
Whose might hath perfection of beauty outwrought,
Returns the great answer of peace which we sought.

And we know, when the race of the planets is run,
And the day shall no longer behold thee, O Sun!
Our souls shall find light with that Infinite One.

O Source of all Being! whose name everywhere
Is sung in hosannas, or murmured in prayer,
We trust, unreserving, our souls to thy care.

GREATHEART AND GIANT DESPAIR.

"Then said Mr. Greatheart, 'I have a commandment to resist sin, to overcome evil, to fight the good fight of faith; and I pray, with whom should I fight this good fight, if not with Giant Despair?'

"Now Giant Despair, because he was a giant, thought no man could overcome him; and again thought he, 'Since heretofore I have made a conquest of angels, shall Greatheart make me afraid?' So he harnessed himself and went out. Then they fought for their lives, and Giant Despair was brought to the ground, but was loth to die. He struggled hard, and had, as they say, as many lives as a cat; but Greatheart was his death, for he left him not till he had severed his head from his shoulders."
BUNYAN'S PILGRIM'S PROGRESS.

HAVE you heard of that marvelous story,
   That wonderful romance of old,
The story of Christian, the pilgrim,
   So quaintly and earnestly told?
'Tis a curious dream, with a beautiful gleam
   Of light through its mystery thrown;
'Tis a picture of life, where the Soul in its strife
   With the demons of darkness is shown.
Nor yet have the indolent ages
   Its mystical meaning outgrown.

Dark threads from the loom of old Error
  Are shot through its fabric of light,
Yet its blendings of Beauty and Terror
  Are wrought with a masterly might.
The gleam and the glare of Destruction are there,
  With demons the soul to appall;
And the pitfalls of Death, with their sulphurous breath,
  Where the weak and unwary must fall.
But, ah! shall we call these mere fancies?
  Life yet hath a meaning for all.

And there in that wonderful region,
  With battlements blackened and bare,
To the sorrow of Hopeful and Christian,
  Stood the Castle of Giant Despair;
For they ventured to stray in a perilous way,
  Where the Giant was searching about,
Who seized on these men, and into a den,
  'Neath his gloomy old Castle of Doubt,
He thrust the poor sorrowful pilgrims,
  'Neath that dismal old Castle of Doubt.

It was said that he came "with a cudgel,"
  And he beat them from day to day,
Till they chanced on "The Key of Promise,"
  When they fled from his wrath away.

Then with friendly design they made ready a sign,
   And they placed it with pious care
O'er the perilous way where they went astray,
   That pilgrims might ever beware
Of the dangers of Doubting Castle,
   And the wrath of old Giant Despair.

Thereafter came Greatheart the valiant,
   Unrivaled in courage and might,
The friend of the weak and defenseless,
   Who had pledged his good sword to the Right.
There, boldly defiant, he challenged the Giant
   From his stronghold of Death to come out;
And Giant Despair, with an insolent air,
   Looked down from the Castle of Doubt,
And cried, "I will slay thee, vile braggart,
   And put all thy forces to rout."

Then in haste he came down from his Castle,
   With his terrible breastplate of fire,
And straight upon Greatheart the valiant,
   He rushed with impetuous ire.
But nothing dismayed, with his keen, trusty blade
   Greatheart smote the old Giant amain,
Firm, fearless, and fast, until vanquished at last,
   He struggled and died on the plain.
Yet 'tis said, that far down in the ages,
   He came to existence again.

Do you deem this an idle old story,
　　Dragged out from the dust of the Past?
Alas! though so time-worn and hoary,
　　Its truths in the Present stand fast.
High up in the air, all blackened and bare,
　　Still rises the Castle of Doubt,
And the Giant, I trow, should you seek for him now,
　　You would find him still prowling about;
And the souls who go in to his Castle,
　　Are more than the souls who come out.

With the cudgel of Old Tradition,
　　Does he beat them from day to day,
And he carefully hides from their vision
　　The Light of the Present away.
The angels above, with compassionate love,
　　A plan for their rescue devise;
But the Giant cries out from his Castle of Doubt,
　　"Beware of delusion and lies!"
So they shrink back again to their prison,
　　And fear through the Truth to grow wise.

O, where is our Greatheart the valiant!
　　A terrible warfare to wage
On this old Theological Giant,
　　The Doubt and Despair of this age?

Let us rise, one and all, when our leader shall call,
  And each for the conflict prepare;
We will march round about that old Castle of Doubt,
  With our "Banner of Light" on the air,
And raze to its very foundations
  The stronghold of Giant Despair.

"THE ORACLE."

Like the roar of distant cataracts,
  Like the slumbrous roll of waves,
Like the night-wind in the willows,
  Sighing over lonely graves,
Like oracular responses,
  Echoing from their secret caves,
Comes a sound of solemn meaning
  From the spirits gone before;
Comes a terrible "*awake thou!*"
  Startling man from sleep once more,
Like a wild wave beating, breaking,
  On this Life's tempestuous shore.

In Earth's desolated temples
  Have the oracles grown dumb,
And the priests, with lifeless rituals,
  All man's noblest powers benumb;
But a solemn voice is speaking —
  Speaking of the yet to come.

There will be a chosen priestess,
　Springing from the lap of Ease,
Hastening to the soul's Dodona,
　Where, amid the sacred trees,
She will hear divine responses,
　Whispered in the passing breeze.

She will be a meek-faced woman,
　Chastened by Affliction's rod,
Who hath worshiped at the altar
　Of the spirit's "unknown God;"
Who in want, and woe, and weakness,
　All alone the wine-press trod,
Till the salt sea-foam of Sorrow
　Whitened on her quivering lips,
Till her heart's full tide of anguish
　Flooded to her finger-tips,
And her soul sank down in darkness,
　Smitten by a dread eclipse.

"Pure in heart," and "poor in spirit,"
　Hers will be that inner life,
Which Earth's martyr-souls inherit,
　Who are conquerors in the strife.
Born of God they walk with Angels,
　Where the air with love is rife.

Men will call her "Laureola,"*
    And her pale, meek brow will crown;
But with holiest aspirations,
    She will shun the world's renown,
And before the Truth's high altar,
    Cast Earth's votive offerings down.

Men will sit like little children
    At her feet, high truths to learn,
And for love, the pure and holy,
    She will cause their hearts to yearn;
Then the innocence of Eden
    To their spirits shall return.
Very fearless in her freedom,
    She will scorn to simply please;
But the fiercest lion-spirits
    She will lead with quiet ease.
Calm, but earnest, firm and truthful,
    She will utter words like these:—

"Wherefore, O ye sons of Sorrow!
Do ye idly sit and borrow
Care and trouble for the morrow —
    Filling up your cup with woe?
Leave, O, leave your visions dreary!
Hush your doleful miserére!
    See the lilies how they grow —

---

* The name signifies a small laurel-wreath.

"Bending down their heads so lowly,
As though heaven were far too holy,
Growing patiently and slowly
   To the end that God designed.
In their fragrance and their beauty,
Filling up their sphere of duty —
   Each is perfect in its kind.

"Deeper than all sense of seeing
Lies the secret source of being,
And the soul with Truth agreeing,
   Learns to live in thoughts and deeds.
'For the life is more than raiment,'
And the Earth is pledged for payment
   Unto man, for all his needs.

"Nature is your common mother,
Every living man your brother;
Therefore love and serve each other;
   Not to meet the law's behest,
But because through cheerful giving,
You will learn the art of living,
   And to love and serve is best.

"Life is more than what man fancies —
Not a game of idle chances,
But it steadily advances

·Up the rugged steeps of Time,
Till man's complex web of trouble —
Every sad hope's broken bubble,
　Hath a meaning most sublime.

"More of practice, less profession,
More of firmness, less concession,
More of freedom, less oppression
　In your Church and in your State;
More of life, and less of fashion,
More of love, and less of passion —
　That will make you good and great.

"When true hearts, divinely gifted,
From the chaff of Error sifted,
On their crosses are uplifted,
　Shall your souls most clearly see
That earth's greatest time of trial
Calls for holy self-denial —
　Calls on men to *do* and *be*.

"But, forever and forever,
Let it be your soul's endeavor,
Love from hatred to dissever;
　And in whatsoe'er ye do —
Won by Truth's eternal beauty —
To your highest sense of duty
　Evermore be firm and true.

"THE ORACLE."

"Heavenly messengers descending,
With a patience never ending,
Evermore their strength are lending,
   And will aid you lest you fall.
Truth is an eternal mountain —
Love, a never-failing fountain,
   Which will cleanse and save you all."

List to her, ye worn and weary —
   Hush your heart-throbs, hold the breath,
Lest ye lose one word of wisdom,
   Which the answering spirit saith;
Hear her, O ye blood-stained nations,
   In your holocaust of death!
Lo! your oracles have failed you,
   In the dust your idols fall,
And a mighty hand is writing
   Words of judgment on the wall:
"Ye are weighed within the balance,
   And found wanting" — one and all.

Mournful murmurs, direful discords,
   Greet you from Destruction's night,
For Life's lower stratum, heaving,
   Brings long-buried wrongs to light,
And your souls shall find no refuge,
   Save with the Eternal Right.

In one grand, unbroken phalanx,
  Firm, united, bravely stand,
Faithful in the way of duty,
  Ready at the Truth's command,
And *forever* let your motto
  Be *this*—"GOD AND MY RIGHT HAND!"

MY ANGEL.

Oft from the summer hights of love,
    Along the ways of Time,
The pilgrims of this lower sphere
    Catch gleams of light sublime,
That stream adown the azure way,
    From heaven's unshadowed clime.

There, on the balmy, golden air,
    Celestial music swells,
Like harps Eolian, gently blown,
    Or chime of silver bells —
And there my star, my angel love,
    My spotless lily dwells.

She came to me, when from my soul
    A demon had been cast;
When I had rent the servile chain,
    Which long had held me fast,
And stood erect, in conscious power,
    A strong, free man at last.

The burnt-out fire-crypts of my life
   Had lost their crimson gleam,
And emptied of their baleful glare,
   I walked as in a dream,
With one great purpose in my heart,
   To *be* and not to *seem*.

Life's holiest lesson then was mine,
   For when at peace within,
And I had cleansed my erring heart
   From its foul taint of sin,
That gentle maiden, pure and sweet,
   Like sunshine entered in.

She was my idol — O my God!
   Have angel hearts above,
Through their long line of endless life,
   Such depth of power to love,
As that with which I folded close,
   My tender, trusting dove?

It was not long, for when the flowers
   Upon the green hill-side
Closed their bright eyes to wake no more,
   My own sweet darling died.
The angels oped the shining door,
   And called her from my side.

O, when they laid her form to rest
    Beneath the churchyard sod,
I longed to follow in the way
    Her angel feet had trod;
For, crushed and bruised, my spirit yearned
    To hide itself in God.

Love led me to the inner depth,
    Which sorrow had unsealed,
And there I saw the wealth of power
    Within my soul concealed —
In that dark, desolating hour,
    Life's meaning stood revealed.

I knew myself, and knowing this,
    The power to me was given
To bridge across the dark abyss
    Between my soul and heaven,
And gather up the golden link
    Which seemed so harshly riven.

The angel hand of her I loved
    Was gently laid in mine;
She led me, by a path of peace,
    To Truth's eternal shrine,
Where my glad soul will never cease
    To worship Love Divine.

Thus have I learned how vain are creeds
  Man's reason to control;
His lesser life supplies its needs
  From Life's majestic Whole.
Love is the guiding star to *Love*,
  And *Soul* must speak to *Soul*.

"I ask not for wealth, which would make me a slave;
I ask not a name, to be lost at the grave;
I ask not for glory, for honor, or power;
Or freedom from care through my life's little hour —
But I ask that the gift which hath made thee divine,
Of comfort, and healing, and strength, may be mine."

Then the angel uplifted a chalice most fair,
Which seemed to be filled with a balm-breathing air,
And a chrism outpoured on the suppliant's head,
Whose fragrance like soft wreathing incense outspread.
"Go forth," said the angel, "thy mission fulfill,
With faith in the heart, which gives strength to the will."

Then lo! in an instant the angel had flown,
And left the glad mortal in silence, alone;
But a token was given that his mission was blest,
When the dove fluttered down and reposed in his breast;

As the prophet of old let his mantle of grace
Float downward to him who should stand in his
    place.

O Helper! O Healer! whoever thou art,
Let love, like an angel, abide in thy heart.
Let mercy plead low for the sinful and wrong,
Let might, born of justice and right, make thee
    strong;
Then help shall descend at thy call from above,
And peace in thy bosom shall rest like a dove.

TRUTH TRIUMPHANT.

O YE who dare not trust the Soul
    To guide you in your heavenward way —
Who turn from its divine control,
    Blind Superstition to obey —
Know that at length shall come an hour,
    When darkness shall be changed to light,
And Truth, majestic in her power,
    Shall vindicate her ancient right.

The monstrous blasphemy of creeds
    Which represent an angry God,
Who tempts man sorely through his needs,
    And meets his failings with a rod —
Eternal wrath, through blood appeased,
    The curse of God, salvation's plan,
Are nightmare visions, which have seized
    The slumbering consciousness of man.

Beyond the dim and distant line,
    Which bounds the vision of to-day,
Great stars of truth shall rise and shine
    With steady and unclouded ray;

And calm, brave souls, who through the night
   Have waited patiently and long,
Will see these heralds of the light,
   And feel themselves in truth made strong.

Blind Superstition, cowering, sits
   Amid the ashes of the past;
While old Tradition, bat-like, flits
   Where Time its deepest gloom hath cast.
The bigot, prospering through fraud,
   Pays to the church his tithes, and then,
With pious fervor, thanks the Lord
   That "he is not like other men."

The church, by deep dissensions riven,
   To man's progression shuts the door,
And failing thus to enter heaven,
   The "poor in spirit" walk before.
The blood of millions on her hands —
   She pampers pride and winks at sin —
A whited sepulchre she stands,
   Hiding but dead men's bones within.

We do not ask for forms and creeds,
   Or useless dogmas, old or new,
But we *do* ask for Christian deeds,
   With man's progression full in view.

Let her be first to aid and bless,
  And not the first to cast a stone,
The while her robes of righteousness
  Are over foul corruptions thrown.

The pure, fresh impulse of to-day,
  Which thrills within the human heart,
As time-worn errors pass away,
  Fresh life and vigor shall impart.
New hopes, like beauteous strangers, wait
  An entrance to man's willing breast,
And child-like faith unbars the gate,
  To welcome in each heavenly guest.

The new must e'er supplant the old,
  While Time's unceasing current flows,
Only new beauties to unfold,
  And brighter glories to disclose;
For every crumbling altar-stone
  That falls upon the way of time,
Eternal wisdom hath o'erthrown,
  To build a temple more sublime.

O ye! who dare not trust the soul
  To guide you in the way to heaven,
Remember that the lifeless whole
  Is quickened by the hidden leaven;

And they who, fearlessly and free,
  The rugged hights of life ascend,
With one united voice agree,
  "*It can be trusted to the end.*"

JUBILATE.

BY MISS LIZZIE DOTEN.

(Air—Auld Lang Syne.)

The world has felt a quickening breath
  From Heaven's eternal shore,
And souls triumphant over Death
  Return to earth once more.
For *this* we hold our jubilee,
  For this with joy we sing—
"O Grave! where is thy victory?
  O Death! where is thy sting?"

Our cypress wreaths are laid aside
  For amaranthine flowers,
For Death's cold wave does not divide
  The souls we love from ours.
From pain, and death, and sorrow free,
  They join with us to sing—
"O Grave! where is thy victory?
  O Death! where is thy sting?"

"Sweet spirits, welcome yet again!"
  With loving hearts we cry;
And "Peace on earth, good will to men,"
  The angel hosts reply.
From doubt and fear, through truth made free,
  With faith triumphant sing—
"O Grave! where is thy victory?
  O Death! where is thy sting?"

This Ode was sung at Boston Music Hall, on March 31, 1868, it being the Twentieth Anniversary of Modern Spiritualism. It is now reissued by the Shawmut Spiritual Lyceum, and the audience is invited to join in the singing.

March, 31, 1881.

GOOD IN ALL.

'Tis a beautiful thought, by Philosophy taught,
That from all things created some good is outwrought;
That each is for use, and not one for abuse,
Which leaves the transgressor no room for excuse.

Thus the great, and the small, and the humblest of all,
To action and duty alike have a call;
And he does the best, who excels all the rest,
In making the lot of humanity blest.

As Jonathan Myer sat one night by the fire,
Watching the flames from the embers expire,
O'er his senses there stole, and into his soul,
A spell of enchantment he could not control.

The wind shook his door, and a terrible roar
In his chimney was heard, like the waves on the shore.

In wonder, amazed, old Jonathan gazed
At the huge oaken back-log as fiercely it blazed.

The flames of his fire leaped higher and higher,
And out of its brightness looked images dire;
Till at length, a great brand straight on end
    seemed to stand,
And then into human proportions expand.

Old Jonathan said, with a shake of his head,
"There's nothing in nature I've reason to dread,
For my conscience is clear, and I'd not have a
    fear,
Should Satan himself at this moment appear."

"Ha! your words shall be tried," quick the demon
    replied,
"For, lo! *I am Satan*, here, close by your side.
Men should never defy such a being as I,
For when they least think it, behold I am nigh."

Said Jonathan Myer, as he stirred up the fire,
"Your face nor your figure I do not admire;
But if that is your style, why, it isn't worth while
For me to find fault or your Maker revile.

"Now don't have a fear, lest it should appear
That you're an intruder — I welcome you here!

So pray take a seat, and warm up your feet,
For I think I have heard that you're partial to heat."

"Well, you are either a fool or remarkably cool,"
Said Satan — accepting the low wooden stool —
"But before I depart, I will give you a start
Which will send back the blood with a rush to your heart."

"Well, and what if you should? It might do me good,
For a shock sometimes helps one — so I've understood.
But just here let me say, that for *many* a day
I've been hoping and wishing you'd happen this way.

"So give us your hand, and you'll soon understand,
What a work in the future for you I have planned."
Satan's hand he then seized, which he forcibly squeezed,
At which the arch fiend looked more angry than pleased.

A puzzled surprise looked out of his eyes,
Which was really quite strange for the "Father
    of Lies."
"Come," said he, "this won't do — *I* am Satan,
    not *you.*"
Said Jonathan Myer, "Very true, very true.

"Now don't get perplexed, excited or vexed,
At what I'm about to present to you next.
Your attention please lend, and you'll see in the end,
That Jonathan Myer, at least, is your friend.

"I've been led to suppose, in spite of your foes,
That you are far better than any one knows.
Now, if there is good, in stock, stone, or wood,
I'm bound to get at it, as every one should.

"So I'll not have a fear — though you seem sort
    o' queer —
But what all your goodness will shortly appear.
Fact — I know that it will, though 'tis mingled
    with ill.
So — so — don't get restless — be patient — sit
    still.

"Now I long since agreed, that there was great need
Of a Devil and Hell in the Orthodox creed.

All things are for use, and none for abuse,
(And the same law applies to a man or a goose.)

"So they'll keep you in play till the Great Judgment Day,
When the Saviour of sinners will thrust you away.
But then, don't you see, they and I don't agree;
So you'll not be obliged to play Satan to me.

"Even now, in your eyes, does there slowly arise
A look, which no lover of good can despise.
So open your heart and its goodness impart,
For now there's no need you should practice your art."

O, strange to relate! all that visage of hate,
Which wore such a fearful expression of late,
Grew gentle and mild as the face of a child,
Ere the springs of its life have with doubt been defiled.

And a voice, soft and low as a rivulet's flow,
Said gently, " I was but in seeming your foe.
Man ever will find, in himself or his kind,
Either evil or good, as he makes up his mind.

" As God is in all, so he answered your call,
And the evil appearance to you is let fall.

This truth I commend to your soul as a friend,
That evil will *all* change to good in the end."

Then Jonathan Myer sat *alone* by his fire,
Till he saw the last light from the embers expire,
And he thoughtfully said, as he turned toward his bed,
"I will banish all hate and put love in its stead."

"I will *do*, and not *dream*—I will *be*, and not *seem*,
And the triumph of goodness I'll take for my theme.
Great Spirit above! I have learned through thy love,
That the Serpent has uses as well as the Dove."

JOHN ENDICOTT.

"If ye love me, keep my commandments."—JESUS.

TRUTH hath no need of outward sign,
    To hold her calm, resistless sway —
No symbol, howsoe'er divine,
    Can rule the conscience of to-day.
And he who, scorning praise or blame,
    Stays not to kneel before the cross,
But serves the Truth through flood and flame,
    Shall win the crown, nor suffer loss.

Back to the old heroic Past,
    With reverent hearts, our gaze we turn —
From souls proved faithful to the last,
    A lesson for to-day we learn.
Once more, as from a master's hand,
    Upon life's canvass glows the scene —
Once more behold that little band
    Of valiant men on Salem green.

Had they not left the friends of youth,
   Their childhood's home, their fathers' graves,
That they might worship God in truth,
   And be no more a tyrant's slaves?
Still followed fast the royal wrath;
   And as they marched with measured tread,
Casting its shadow o'er their path,
   The tyrant's flag waved over head.

"Halt!" said the brave John Endicott,
   With knitted brow and eyes aflame;
"Halt! — Forward! Ensign Davenport!
   Down with that flag! in God's high name!"
Down drooped the flag, whose folds of blood
   Seemed like the Parcæ's web of fate,
Whereon the cross so long had stood
   For tyranny in Church and State.

He raised his hand, and sternly tore
   The red cross from its field of blue;
Then nerved with fire his arm upbore,
   And held the fragment full in view.
"Now by the homage that we pay
   To God the Father, God the Son,
May righteous Heaven approve this day
   The deed that my right hand hath done."

"To Him whose law hath all sufficed,
  Be power and glory evermore,
But this cursed sign of Anti-Christ
  Shall not profane this hallowed shore."
One moment — and a hush like death —
  Then flashed the fire from every eye,
And like the tempest's sudden breath,
  A shout tumultuous rent the sky.

Those ranks of stern, heroic men,
  Who asked no favor, knew no fear,
Could "beard the lion in his den,"
  When duty made the pathway clear,
There in the howling wilderness,
  In holy triumph did they sing,
"Christ is our refuge in distress,
  The Lord of Hosts alone is King."

Linked, by the lengthening years of time,
  To all that grand heroic past,
The mantle of their faith sublime
  Is on this generation cast.
Whene'er the cross no longer stands
  For freedom, faith, and love divine,
Men tear it down with willing hands,
  And worship God without the sign.

John Endicott! John Endicott!
  Thine earthly victory is won,
But valiant still, and swerving not,
  Thy steadfast soul "is marching on."
Like thee we would be brave and true,
  And fearless in the faith abide,
That souls who nobly dare and do,
  Have God and Heaven upon their side.

THE TRIUMPH OF FREEDOM.

REJOICE! O blood-stained Nation, in darkness
wandering long,
For Freedom is triumphant, and Right hath conquered Wrong.
To-day, the glorious birthright the patriot Fathers
gave,
Makes, through Eternal Justice, a freeman of the
slave.

And swift the glorious tidings, which rolls majestic on,
Thrills from old Massachusetts to the shores of
Oregon.
The gray old mountain-echoes shout it loudly to
the sea,
And the wild winds join the chorus in the "anthem
of the free."

For this, the God of nations sealed this land as
sacred soil,
And thenceforth made it holy, with blood, and
sweat, and toil.

For this, the lonely Mayflower spread her white
    wings to the breeze,
And bore the Pilgrim Fathers across the stormy
    seas.

For this, the blood of patriots baptized old Bunker
    Hill,
And Lexington and Concord made known the *people's will.*
For this, both Saratoga and Yorktown's fields were
    won,
And Fame's unfading laurels wreathed the brow
    of Washington.

For this, your glorious Channing plead on the
    "weaker side,"
And Parker, brave and fearless, sought to stem Oppression's tide.
For this, the lips of Phillips burned with Athenian
    fire,
Till every flaming sentence leapt forth in righteous
    ire.

And Garrison, the dauntless, declared, "I will be
    heard!"
O thou sturdy, war-worn veteran! well hast thou
    kept thy word!

Thou hast sent the foul Hyena howling fiercely to his den,
And thy battle-cry was "Freedom!" till the cannon said, "Amen!"

For this, like royal Cæsar, within the Senate Hall,
On the noble head of Sumner did the blows of Slavery fall;
For this, that band of heroes, with their Spartan chief, John Brown,
As a sacrifice to Freedom, their precious lives laid down.

And for this you bore and suffered, "till forbearance ceased to be
A virtue," and High Heaven called on you to be free.
Then, once more, the blood of heroes leaped like fire within each vein,
And the long-slumbering Lion rose, and, wrathful, shook his mane.

O! the page of future history shall, with truthful record, tell
How you met the fearful issue, how bravely and how well;

How you gave uncounted treasure from out your
    toil-won hoard,
And how, as free as water, heroic blood was
    poured;—

How Grant, with stern persistence, smote the foe-
    men day by day;
How Sheridan and Sherman urged their victorious
    way;
How Farragut and Porter swept triumphant o'er
    the sea,
And how the gallant Winslow won *his* glorious
    victory;—

And alas! how noble Ellsworth fell in his youth-
    ful pride,
And Winthrop, Baker, Lyon, for Freedom bled and
    died;
And true, brave hearts unnumbered, before the can-
    non's breath,
On the wild, red sea of slaughter, swept down the
    tide of death;—

And how, amid the tumult, in every battle
    pause,
Was heard the cry for "Justice to the bondman
    and his cause."

O! your fathers' slumbering ashes cried, "Amen!"
    from out each grave,
When your grand old Constitution gave freedom
    to the slave.

And, as the glorious tidings upon the nation
    fell,
Satan, with all his legions, went howling down to
    Hell.
Of crime and blood no longer could he freely
    drink his fill,
For the curséd demon, Slavery, had best performed
    his will.

Let words of deep thanksgiving blend with the
    tears you shed
For the hosts of noble martyrs who in Freedom's
    cause have bled.
Though they fell before the sickle which reaps the
    battle-plain,
Yet, to-day, they know in heaven, that they perished not in vain.

Your nation's glorious Eagle, with an unfaltering
    flight,
Hath perched at length, in triumph, on Freedom's
    loftiest height;

The stars upon your banner burn with a fairer
    flame,
And the radiant stripes no longer are emblems of
    your shame.

The slave, made like his master, "in the image of
    his God,"
Shall bare his back no longer to the oppressor's
    rod;
His night of pain and anguish, of want and woe,
    has past,
And Freedom's radiant morning has dawned on
    him at last.

O thou Recording Angel! turn to that page
    whereon
Is traced, in undimmed brightness, the name of
    Washington,
And, with thy pen immortal, in characters of
    flame,
To stand henceforth and ever, write also Lincoln's
    name!

The first hurled back the tyrant, in the country's
    hour of need,
The last, divinely guided, hath made her free in-
    deed.

Let a nation's grateful tribute to each, alike, be given,
While the kingdom, power and glory are ascribed alone to Heaven.

"Ethiopia no longer stretcheth forth her hands" in vain;
On the demon of oppression she hath left her servile chain;
Then swell the shout of triumph, till the nations hear afar;
Three cheers — three cheers for Freedom! Huzzä! Huzzä! Huzzä!

OUR SOLDIERS' GRAVES.

Sons of the nation to glory restored,
   Strew with fresh laurels the patriot's grave —
Heed the libation to Liberty poured —
   Honor the blood of the fearless and brave.

When the red bolts of destruction were hurled,
   Bursting in tempests of fury and flame,
Faithful to Freedom, the hope of the world,
   Swift to the rescue each patriot came.

Breasting the waves of the battle's wild sea,
   Facing, unflinching, the cannon's hot breath,
Hail to the brave! who marched fearless and free,
   Down to the valley and shadow of Death.

Trace it in marble as white as the snows,
   Chisel in granite the record sublime,
Sacred to Freedom — and teaching our foes
   Lessons of wisdom as lasting as time.

Bright as the stars in the firmament shine,
    Still may they watch o'er this land from on high,
Teaching our hearts, as their names we enshrine,
    Faithful to Freedom to live and to die.

OUTWARD BOUND.

It was midnight dark, when I launched my bark
   On a wild, tempestuous sea;
The lightnings flashed, and the white waves dashed
   Like steeds from the rein set free.
'Twas a fearful night, and no beacon-light
   O'er the waste of waters shone;
On the wide, wide sweep of the angry deep,
   Alas! I was all alone.

I had left behind the faithful and kind,
   The gentle and true of heart;
O God above! from their clinging love,
   It was hard, it was hard to part.
O, why did I leave such hearts to grieve,
   And haste from my home away?
'Twas the chosen hour of a mighty power,
   Whose summons I must obey.

I had heard the call which must come to all,
   And I felt, by my quickened breath,
I must leave that shore to return no more,
   For the name of that sea was Death.

Thus Outward Bound, with a dizzy sound
  Like waves in my troubled brain,
I drifted away like a soul astray,
  For I felt that to strive was vain.

Like the brooding wing of some grewsome thing,
  The darkness around me spread;
The wild winds roared, and the tempests poured
  Their fury upon my head.
Anon through the night, like serpents bright,
  The quivering lightnings came,
Or an instant coiled where the white waves boiled,
  To moisten their tongues of flame.

In the giddy whirl, in the greedy swirl,
  I felt I was sinking fast,
When an arm, as white as the opal bright,
  Was firmly around me cast.
And a well-known voice made my heart rejoice—
  "Fear not! for the strife is o'er;
To your resting-place in my warm embrace,
  Do I welcome you back once more."

'Twas my mother dear spake those words of cheer,
  Whom I met with a glad surprise,
For I thought she slept where the willows wept,
  Till the day when the dead should rise.

I had passed away from my form of clay,
    But not to a distant sphere;
Like a troubled dream did the struggle seem,
    For my spirit still lingered here.

I had weathered the storm, but my mortal form
    Like a wreck in my presence lay;
They said I was dead when my spirit fled,
    And with weeping they turned away.
Then the dearest came, and she sobbed my name;
    But how could those pale lips speak?
She bent o'er my form like a reed in the storm,
    As she kissed my clay-cold cheek.

I was with her there, and with tender care
    I folded her close to my breast,
Till the heart's wild throb, and the bursting sob,
    Were silenced and soothed to rest.
O human love! there is nought above,
    That ever will rudely part
The sacred tie, or the union high,
    Of those who are one in heart.

A bridge leads o'er from the heavenly shore,
    Where the happy spirits pass,
And the angels that stand with the harp in the hand,
    On the "sea, as it were, of glass,"

Play so soft and clear that the human ear,
    And the spirits who love the Lord,
Can catch the sound through the space profound,
    And join in the sweet accord.

O, what is death? 'Tis a fleeting breath —
    A simple but blessèd change —
'Tis rending a chain, that the soul may gain
    A higher and broader range.
Unbounded space is its dwelling-place,
    Where no human foot hath trod,
But everywhere doth it feel the care
    And the changeless love of God.

O, then, though you weep when your loved ones sleep,
    When the rose on the cheek grows pale,
Yet their forms of light, just concealed from sight,
    Are only behind the vail.
With their faces fair, and their shining hair
    With blossoms of beauty crowned,
They will also stand, with a helping hand,
    When you shall be Outward Bound.

THE WANDERER'S WELCOME HOME.

A woman, with weary heart and hand,
   Wasted and worn by the rude world's strife,
Prayed for the peace of the better land,
   And the mansions fair of the higher life.
She prayed at night in the churchyard lone,
Resting her brow on a cold, white stone.

All of that day in the public street,
   She had played on her harp and patiently sung,
Till the cold wind palsied her weary feet,
   And chilled the words on her faltering tongue.
And but one penny to meet her need
Had the cold world spared from its selfish greed.

O, the mocking words of "Home, sweet home,"
   Had she sung for that paltry, pitiful fee,
She who thus lonely was doomed to roam,
   While never a home on earth had she;
But often the lips must perform a part
That is foreign and false to the aching heart.

At night, by her sorrowful longings led,
   She had turned from the dwellings of men away,
And sought the place of the sleeping dead,
   In silence and darkness alone to pray.
While her harp, as it sighed in the wintry air,
Seemed to echo the tone of her lone heart's prayer.

Her face was white as the drifted snows,
   And her eyes were fixed in a dull despair,
As if the chilling tide of her woes
   Had swelled from her heart, and had frozen there.
She lifted her hands to the wintry sky,
And prayed in her anguish, "Lord, let me die!"

Then soft and clear to her quickened sense
   A vision of heavenly beauty came;
Her spirit thrilled with a joy intense,
   And her heart grew warm with a heavenly flame.
Sweet voices were singing, "No longer roam,
But haste to the joys of thy 'home, sweet home.'"

The stars looked down from the wintry skies
   In solemn beauty, undimmed and clear,
But the vision that greeted her eager eyes
   Was unto her spirit both warm and near.
Again those voices poured forth the lay,
"To thy 'home, sweet home,' O, haste away."

She seized her harp, and her white hand swept
  With a full accord o'er its trembling strings,
Waking the echoes that round her slept,
  Like the swan, which in dying so sweetly sings,
As she answered them back, "No more to roam,
Lo! I come, I come to my 'home, sweet home.'"

The watchman who went on his lonely round
  Felt his stout heart thrill with a sense of dread,
When he heard that strange and unwonted sound
  Come forth from the place of the silent dead.
He listened, and breathed a fervent prayer
For the rest of the dreamless sleepers there.

The watchman who went on his lonely round
  Remembered that sound at break of day,
And he turned aside to the hallowed ground,
  Where the dead in their quiet slumbers lay.
And there he found, by the cold, white stone,
The lifeless form whence the soul had flown.

With white lips parted, and eyes upraised,
  And her hands to the harp-strings frozen cold,
The warm blood chilled in his veins as he gazed,
  And he thought of the weight of her woes untold.
"Great God!" he said, "is our faith a lie,
That thus, unheeded, thy children die!"

"Hush, murmuring spirit!" the Truth replied;
  "Loss ever walks hand in hand with gain;
Life hath its sunny and shady side,
  Its major, as well as its minor strain.
And she who thus lonely was doomed to roam
Now rests at peace in her 'home, sweet home."

"The pilgrims of earth, in their homeward way,
  Full often in danger and doubt must stand;
But out of the darkness shall come the day,
  And strength and healing from God's right hand.
And the scales of life, as they rise and fall,
Full measures of justice shall mete to all."

LABOR AND WAIT.

ALL green, and bitter, and hard, and sour,
   The fruit on the Tree of Life is growing;
But the genial sunshine, with quickening power,
   Will sweeten its juices like nectar flowing.
For the full, fair growth of its perfect state
   There is only needed the right condition.
Then labor and wait, both early and late,
   Till the ripening future shall bring fruition.

Far out in the harvest fields of Time,
   The grain for the reaper is standing ready,
And they who come to the work sublime
   Must toil with a patience calm and steady.
Truth never was subject to Chance or Fate —
   Its sickle, so sharp, cuts clean and even.
Then labor and wait, both early and late,
   For the seed-field of Earth yields the harvest of Heaven.

In their quiet graves, on the green hill-side,
   The sacred dust of your loved is sleeping;
And the homes where the light of their smile has died
   Are filled with the sorrowful sounds of weeping.
But over the gloomy clouds of Fate,
   The light of the better land is shining;
Then labor and wait, both early and late,
   For the cloud of Death has a silver lining.

There are fair, sweet faces, and gentle eyes,
   That look through the shadows and mists above you;
And the fond affection that never dies,
   Still speaks from the lips of the blest who love you.
They call you up from your low estate,
   To the boundless bliss of the life supernal.
Then labor and wait, both early and late,
   For Time is short, but Life is Eternal.

FRAE RHYMING ROBIN.

The following poem was given under the inspiration of Robert Burns, at the close of a lecture on " The Immaculate Conception."

Guid Friends:
    I will na' weave my rhymes to-night
        In winsome measure,
    Or strive your fancies to delight
        Wi' songs o' pleasure;
    But gin [1] ye hae na' heard too much
        O' solemn preachin',
    I'll gie ye just anither touch
        O' useful teachin'.

    But, aiblins,[2] when ye hear my verse,
        Ye may be thinkin'
    That I hae sunk frae bad to warse,
        And still am sinkin';
    But though I seem to fa' from grace,
        In man's opinion,
    Auld Hornie ne'er will see my face
        In his dominion.

[1] If.   [2] Perhaps.

An unco [1] change will come, ere lang,
    O'er all your dreamin',
And ye shall see that right and wrang
    Are much in seemin'.
Man shall na' langer perjure love,
    Nor think it treason
Anent [2] the mighty King above,
    To use his reason.

Ay, love and nature, frae the first,
    Hae been perverted,
And man, frae Adam, will be cursed,
    Till he's converted:
For Nature will avenge her cause
    On ilka [3] creature,
Who will na' take her, wi' her laws,
    For guide and teacher.

Auld Custom is a sleekit [4] saint,
    And sae is Fashion,
And baith will watch till sinners faint,
    To lay the lash on;
Men follow them wi' ane accord,
    Led by their noses,
Because they cry, "Thus saith the Lord,
    The God o' Moses."

[1] Very great.   [2] Against.   [3] Every.   [4] Cunning.

The time will come when man will ken
    God's word far better;
He'll live mair in the spirit then,
    Less in the letter;
And that which man ance called impure,
    Through partial seein',
He'll find for it baith cause and cure,
    In his ain bein'.

Man needna' gae to auld lang syne
    For truth to guide him,
For if he seeks, he sure will fin'
    Truth close beside him.
Each gowan[1] is ordained o' grace
    To be his teacher,
And ilka toddlin' weanie's[2] face
    Is text and preacher.

Man was na' born a child o' hell
    Frae his creation:
The love that made him will itsel'
    Be his salvation.
Each child that's born o' perfect love
    Can be man's saviour:
Love is his warrant frae above,
    For guid behavior.

[1] Daisy.   [2] Each tottering child.

His mither may be high or low,
　　A Miss or Madam;
The God within him will outgrow
　　The sin o' Adam;
His only bed may be the earth,
　　His hame a shealin';[1]
It will na' change his real worth,
　　Or inward feelin'.

Though born beneath the Church's ban,
　　Or man's displeasure,
He will na' be the less a man
　　In mind or measure.
God's image, stamped upon his brow,
　　Is his defender,
And makes him — as ye hae it now —
　　"Guid legal tender."

But ilka child that's born o' hate —
　　However lawful —
Will be the victim, sune or late,
　　O' passions awful;
Will hirple[2] o'er the ways o' life,
　　Wi' friends scarce ony,
And in the dour[3] warld's angry strife,
　　Find faes full mony.

[1] Humble cot.　　[2] Walk crazily.　　[3] Contrary.

The Power aboon, sae kind and guid,
    Who ever sees us,
Will gie to men, whene'er they need,
    A John or Jesus.
The sin o' Adam will na' cause
    His love to vary,
Nor need he change creation's laws [1]
    To form a Mary.

Man's sympathies must largely share
    In what is human,
And he will love the truth the mair,
    That's born o' woman.
The De'il himsel', at last, through love
    Will be converted,
And, reckoned wi' the saunts above,
    Leave hell deserted.

The One who laid Creation's plan
    Knows how to end it,
Nor need he ever call on man
    To help him mend it.
Then, syne [2] this Being is your friend,
    And man your brither,
Gae on rejoicing to the end,
    Wi' ane anither.

---

[1] Referring to the dogma of the Immaculate Conception.   [2] Since.

AN ELEGY ON THE DEVIL.

Given under the inspiration of Robert Burns.

MEN say the De'il is dead at last,
   And that his course is ended,
Which sure must be an unco loss
   To those whom he befriended.
No doubt he managed to evade
   The sinner's awful sentence,
By that last trick, so often played,
   Of a death-bed repentance.

Alas! alas! we dinna ken
   What will be done without him,
For all the pious sons of men
   Made such a rant about him.
Whene'er they chanced to gang agley,
   Or did a deed of evil,
Or winked at sin upon "the sly,"
   'Twas all laid to tne Deevel.

But henceforth they must bear their sin,
  And come to the confession,
Without a single hope to win
  A pardon for transgression;
Unless, indeed, they try the plan
  Of wise old Orthodoxy,
Invented for puir sinful man,
  O' saving souls by proxy.

But hoolie! what a grand mistake
  Was made at the creation,
That God should e'er a De'il make,
  To peril men's salvation.
He might have made puir man, nae doubt,
  To grace a greater debtor,
Had he but left the De'il out,
  Or only made man better.

I wad na mock at honest faith,
  Or utter thought profanely,
But then 'tis better for us baith,
  That truth be spoken plainly.
The great, guid God, who loves us a',
  Is sure misrepresented,
Whene'er men say he cursed us a'
  In what he could prevented.

And as for Hornie — Nickie-ben —
　　Auld cloven-foot or Deevil, —
I dinna think that he has been,
　　The cause o' all man's evil.
Now that the puir old soul is gone,
　　He does na' seem so hateful,
And those who live, his loss to mourn,
　　Should speak na' word ungrateful.

The clergy, sure, have lost a friend
　　Who never had a rival —
And henceforth all their hopes must end,
　　O' raising a revival.
For when a rout and rant they made,
　　To turn puir souls frae error,
The De'il was half their stock in trade,
　　To fill men's hearts wi' terror.

The politicians might as weel
　　Gie o'er each vain endeavor —
What unco sorrow must they feel,
　　Now he is gone forever!
In all their dealings, hand in hand,
　　They went with him thegither,
They executed what he planned,
　　And each helped on the ither.

And then the long-faced, praying saints,
   Who worshiped God on Sunday,
And set aside their pious feints,
   To serve the De'il on Monday —
They evermore, with empty word,
   Professed their hate of evil;
But while they cried "Guid Lord! Guid Lord,"
   They said aside, "Guid Devil!"

We dinna ken what caused his death,
   Or ended his probation,
Whether it was that he lacked breath,
   Or lacked appreciation.
Perhaps the "origin o' Sin"
   Has proved too tough a question;
He took it for his meat within,
   And died o' indigestion.

Farewell! farewell! auld Nickie-ben;
   We trust ye are forgiven,
For doubtless ye made haste to men',[1]
   And make your peace wi' heaven.
We leave your burial, guid or bad,
   To Truth, as undertaker,
And your puir soul, such as ye had,
   Commend unto its Maker.

[1] Mend.

FRATERNITY.

Could ye but ken, ye sons o' men,
    How truly ye are brithers,
Ye'd make guid speed to stand agreed,
    Tho' born o' various mithers.
Ane common breath, ane common death,
    Ane hame in Heaven above ye —
Ye are the fruit frae one great root
    In the guid God who lo'es ye.

All high and low, all empty show,
    All envious differences,
Will fade from sight and vanish quite,
    When men come to their senses.
Each living man works out the plan
    For which he was intended,
And he does best, who will na' rest
    Until his work is ended.

Your neebors' blame, or sinful shame,
    Should gie your soul na' pleasure,
For while ye judge, wi' cruel grudge,
    You fill your ain sad measure.

The De'il himsel' could scarcely tell
    Which o' ye was the better;
He wad be laith to leave ye baith,
    While either was his debtor.

Here in life's school wi' pain and dool,[1]
    You get your education,
While mony a trip and sinful slip
    Helps on the soul's salvation.
The unco skeigh,[2] wi' heads full high,
    Wha feel themselves maist holy,
Oft learn through sin how to begin
    True life amang the lowly.

Baith you and I may gang agley,[3]
    For 'tis a common failin';
But hauld away! we need na' stay
    A weepin' and a wailin'.
The God aboon cares not how soon
    We leave our sins behind us;
He does not hate us in that state,
    Nor set the De'il to mind us.

And as for Hell, o' which men tell,
    I'm sure o' the opinion,
There's na' such place o' "saving grace"
    In all the Lord's dominion.

---

[1] Sorrow.   [2] Very proud.   [3] Go astray.

And those who rave, puir souls to save,
   Wi' long-faced, pious fleechin',[1]
Will find far hence, that *common sense*
   Is better than *such* preachin'.

That which ye ca' the power o' law,
   Is but a puir invention;
It counts the deed as evil seed,
   But winks at the intention.
Could men but be mair truly free,
   In some things less restrickéd,
The world wad find the human kind
   Wad na' be half sae wicked.

The pent-up steed kept short o' feed
   Is wildest in his roamin';
And dammed-up streams, wi' angry gleams,
   Dash o'er each hindrance foamin'.
Therefore (I pray take what I say
   In spirit, not in letter)
Mankind should be like rivers, free —
   The less they're damned the better.

You need na' heed the grousome creed
   Which tells ye o' God's anger;
On Nature's page frae age to age,
   His love is written stranger.

[1] Praying.

God's providence, in ony sense,
   Has never been one-sided,
And for the weal o' chick, or chiel,
   He amply has provided.

The winter's snaw, the birken shaw,[1]
   The gowans[2] brightly springing,
The murky night, the rosy light,
   The laverocks[3] gayly singing,
The spring's return, the wimplin burn,[4]
   The cushat[5] fondly mated,
All join to tell how unco well
   God lo'es all things created.

Then dinna strive to live and thrive
   Sae selfish and unthinkin',
But firmly stand, and lend a hand
   To keep the weak frae sinkin'.
'Tis love can make, for love's sweet sake,
   A trusty fier[6] in sorrow,
Wha spends his gear[7] wi'out a fear
   O' what may be to-morrow.

The preachers say, there's far awa'
   A land o' milk and honey,
Where all is free as barley brie,
   And wi'out price or money;

---

[1] Birchen grove.   [2] Flowers.   [3] Larks.   [4] Running brooks.
[5] Dove.   [6] Friend.   [7] Money.

But *here* the meat o' love is sweet,
    For souls in sinful blindness,
And there's a milk that's guid for ilk [1] —
    "The milk o' human kindness."

The lift aboon [2] will welcome sune
    The wayworn and the weary,
And angels fair will greet them there,
    Sae winsome and sae cheery.
But while they stay, make smooth the way,
    Through all life's wintry weather,
Until ane bield [3]. and common shield,
    Shall hauld ye all thegither.

[1] Each.   [2] Heaven above.   [3] Shelter.

OWEENA.

Once, when Death, the mighty hunter,
Bent his bow and sent an arrow
Through the shadows of the forest,
Harming not the Bear or Panther,
Harming not the Owl or Raven,
In the bosom of Oweena,
Fairest of the Indian maidens,
Was the fatal arrow hidden.

On the lodge of Massa-wam-sett
Fell a deep and dreadful shadow;
He, the wise and warlike Sachem,
Mourned in silence for Oweena;
But the mother, Nah-me-o-ka,
Like a tall pine in the tempest,
Tossed her arms in wildest anguish,
Pouring forth her lamentation:

"Neen wo-ma-su! Neen wo-ma-su![1]
O my darling! my Oweena!
Mat-ta-neen won-ka-met na-men —[2]
    I shall never see thee more!

"Ho-bo-mo-co, evil Spirit,
Hiding darkly in the forest,
Making shadow in the sunshine,
    You have stolen her away.

"She was like the flowers in spring time,
She was like the singing waters,
She was like the summer sunshine,
    Neen wo-ma-su! She is dead!

"Hear me! Hear me, O Great Spirit!
I will bring thee Bear and Bison,
I will bring thee Beads and Wampum;
    Wilt thou give her back to me?

"Neen wo-ma-su! Neen wo-ma-su!
O my darling! My Oweena!
Mat-ta-neen won-ka-met na-men,
    I shall never see thee more!"

---

[1] My darling.
[2] I shall never see thee more.

Ceaseless was her plaintive wailing,
Even when the fair Oweena
Slept beneath the pine trees' shadow,
In the green and silent forest,
Where the birds sang in the branches,
Where the roses of the summer,
And the vines, with slender fingers,
Clasped their loving hands above her.

From the lodge of Massa-wam-sett,
While the brave old chieftain slumbered,
In the silence of the midnight,
To the grave stole Nah-me-o-ka,
Pouring forth her lamentations:
"Neen wo-ma-su! Neen wo-ma-su!
Mat-ta-neen won-ka-met na-men,
I shall never see thee more!"

Once, the tempest, on its war-path,
Painted all the sky with blackness,
Sped the arrows of the lightning,
And the war-whoop of the thunder,
Made the mighty forest tremble.
But it moved not Nah-me-o-ka,
Only moaning, "Neen wo-ma-su!
I shall never see thee more!"

All the forest leaves were weeping,
And the black wings of the darkness,
Brooding over Nah-me-o-ka,
Filled her with a chilling shudder:
And the thunder seemed to mutter
With a cruel exultation,
"You shall never see her more."
But thereafter came a whisper—

"I am with you, O my mother!
For I cannot turn my footsteps
To the land of the Great Spirit,
While I hear your mournful wailing,
    Calling, calling me again.

"In the hunting-grounds beyond me
There are sunshine, peace and plenty,
But I wander, sad and lonely,
In the land of death and darkness,
    Listening only to your cry.

"Let me go to the Great Spirit,
To the lodge of peace and plenty,
To the land of summer sunshine,
That with life and strength and gladness,
    I may meet you yet again."

Then the soft hand of Oweena
Gently lifted Nah-me-o-ka,
Who with wondering eyes beheld her,
Like a light amid the darkness.
And Oweena safely led her
Through the tempest and the midnight,
To the lodge of Massa-wam-sett,
Kissed her tenderly — and vanished.

From that time did Nah-me-o-ka
Dry her tears, and cease her moaning,
For she said, "I will not keep her
From the land of summer sunshine,
From the home of peace and plenty,
From the lodge of the Great Spirit.
Neen wo-ma-su! Neen wo-ma-su!
In the land of the Hereafter
    I shall meet her yet again."

GONE IS GONE, AND DEAD IS DEAD.

"On returning to the inn, he found there a wandering minstrel — a woman — singing, and accompanying her voice with the music of a harp. The burden of her song was, 'Gone is gone, and dead is dead.' The utter hopelessness of these words filled his soul with anguish. 'O,' he exclaimed, 'thou loved and lost one! patient and long-suffering, would that I could call thee back again, not to forgive me — O, no! — but rather that I might have the consolation of showing thee, by my repentance, how differently I would conduct towards thee now." — JEAN PAUL RICHTER.

"Gone is gone, and dead is dead!"
Words to hopeless sorrow wed —
Words from deepest anguish wrung,
Which a lonely wand'rer sung,
While her harp prolonged the strain,
Like a spirit's cry of pain
When all hope with life is fled:
"Gone is gone, and dead is dead."

Mournful singer! hearts unknown
Thrill responsive to that tone;
By a common weal and woe,
Kindred sorrows all must know.

Lips all tremulous with pain
Oft repeat that sad refrain
When the fatal shaft is sped —
"Gone is gone, and dead is dead."

Pain and death are everywhere —
In the earth, and sea, and air;
And the sunshine's golden glance,
And the heaven's serene expanse,
With a silence calm and high,
Seem to mock that mournful cry
Wrung from hearts by hope unfed —
"Gone is gone, and dead is dead."

O, ye sorrowing ones, arise;
Wipe the tear-drops from your eyes;
Lift your faces to the light;
Read Death's mystery aright.
Life unfolds from life within,
And with death does life begin.
Of the soul can ne'er be said,
"Gone is gone, and dead is dead."

As the stars, which, one by one,
Lit their torches at the sun,
And across ethereal space
Swept each to its destined place,

So the soul's Promethean fire,
Kindled never to expire,
On its course immortal sped,
Is not gone, and is not dead.

By a Power to thought unknown,
Love shall ever seek its own.
Sundered not by time or space,
With no distant dwelling-place,
Soul shall answer unto soul,
As the needle to the pole.
Leaving grief's lament unsaid,
"Gone is gone, and dead is dead."

Evermore Love's quickening breath
Calls the living soul from death;
And the resurrection's power
Comes to every dying hour.
When the soul, with vision clear,
Learns that Heaven is always near,
Never more shall it be said,
"Gone is gone, and dead is dead."

THE SPIRIT TEACHER.

Far in the land of Love and Light,
Where Death's cold touch can never blight
The buds most precious to the sight —
    The Power Divine
Hath given to my fostering care,
A youthful band of spirits fair.
    Thus are they *mine.*

Sweet blossoms from the earthly spring —
Weak fledglings with the untried wing —
Dear lambs — such as the angels bring,
    With tenderest love,
From earthly storms and tempests cold,
Safe to the warm and sheltering fold,
    In heaven above.

O, gentle mothers of the earth,
Who gave these precious spirits birth,
Your homes have lost their sounds of mirth

And childish glee;
But not in Death's embrace they sleep —
Nay, gentle mothers, cease to weep —
    They dwell with me.

There, 'mid the amaranthine bowers,
Through all the long, bright, gladsome hours,
Your loved ones tend their birds and flowers,
    And often come
With gifts of love and garlands bright,
To gladden, with their forms of light,
    Your earthly home.

Their gentle lips to yours are pressed,
Their heads are pillowed on your breast,
And in your loving arms they rest,
    For they are given
By Him whose ways are ever kind,
As precious links of love, to bind
    Your souls to heaven.

O, could the sunshine of the heart
Dispel the blinding tears that start,
And all your doubts and fears depart —
    Those forms, concealed
Like blossoms 'neath the shades of night,
Before your spirit's quickening sight
    Would stand revealed.

They still are yours, and yet are mine;
I teach them of the Life Divine,
And lead them to the truth's pure shrine,
    That evermore,
Through heavenly wisdom understood,
The True, the Beautiful, the Good,
    They may adore.

They know no griefs, they shed no tears,
For perfect love dispels their fears,
And through their life's eternal years,
    They haste to meet
The humblest duty of the way,
And every call of love obey
    With willing feet.

O, ye who tears of anguish shed
Above some empty cradle-bed,
Where once reposed a precious head —
    Be reconciled.
For yet your longing eyes shall see,
In heaven's broad sunshine, glad and free,
    Your spirit child.

They are all there — they are all there —
The young, the beautiful, the fair;
They know no want, they feel no care.

They are not dead;
But quickened in their spirit's powers,
Life crowns with her immortal flowers
    Each shining head.

Some are no longer weak and small,
But fair, and beautiful, and tall;
And yet I call them *children* all,
    For they believe,
With child-like faith, the truths I teach,
And render back in simple speech
    What they receive.

They are more precious in my sight
Than all the radiant gems of light
That on the royal brow of night
    Arise and shine;
And through a pure maternal love,
Known even in the world above,
    I call them mine.

O, ask them not for earth again,
The bitter cup of grief to drain,
To tread in sorrow and in pain
    Life's thorny track.
Love's rainbow arch to heaven they crossed;
Gone, but not dead — unseen, not lost —
    Call them not back.

O, gentle mothers, cease to weep;
The faithful shepherd of the sheep
The tender little lambs will keep.
 'Mid shadows dim,
Lean calmly on the Father's breast —
"He giveth his belovéd rest" —
 Trust ye in him.

LITTLE NELL.

A POEM FOR THE CHILDREN OF THE LYCEUM.

CLEAR the wintry sky was glowing,
Sharp and loud the wind was blowing,
Icy cold the stream was flowing
   In the little woodland dell,
When, with pitcher clasped so tightly,
Tripping cheerfully and lightly,
With her soft eyes smiling brightly,
   To the spring came little Nell.

Late to bed and early rising,
With a patience quite surprising,
And without the least advising,
   Faithful as a little dove —
Thus she toiled for her sick mother,
For, poor child! there was none other,
Not a sister or a brother,
   Who could share her work of love.

As she stooped to dip the water,
Straight the cruel north wind caught her,
Down upon the ground it brought her,
   And the little pitcher fell.
But with merry laugh upspringing,
And again the pitcher bringing,
As she filled it, gayly singing,
   Homeward hastened little Nell.

"Ho!" cried Jack Frost, "if I catch her,
Such cold feet and hands I'll fetch her,
I will make her drop her pitcher —
   Little good-for-nothing thing!
Let me only once get at her,
It will be no trifling matter!
I will make her teeth to chatter
   So, she will not dare to sing."

"Holy angels, guard us ever,
God himself forsakes us never,"
Sung the maiden, blithe as ever —
   "We are his forevermore."
Then the wild wind beating o'er her,
Rudely on her way it bore her,
Heaping up the snow before her,
   Till she reached the cottage door.

Scarcely had her mother missed her.
Hastening quickly to assist her,
Tenderly she stooped and kissed her,
   And the poor, sick mother smiled.
Closely to her heart she pressed her,
Looking up to heaven she blessed her,
And before her God, confessed her
   As His gift — that precious child.

Now, one little word of teaching —
Though I am not fond of preaching —
Yet most earnestly beseeching,
   I would say to children small —
Learn that duties, howe'er lowly,
Done in *love*, will make life holy,
And will bring, though ofttimes slowly,
   Sure and sweet reward to all.

THE SOUL'S DESTINY.

Up o'er the shining ways of light,
   That flash across the starry skies,
Up to Creation's loftiest hight,
   The pathway of the spirit lies.
Where countless constellations gleam,
   The soul triumphant shall ascend,
Shall drink of Life's eternal stream,
   And with new forms of being blend.

No boundless solitude of space
   Shall fill man's conscious soul with awe,
But everywhere his eye shall trace
   The beauty of eternal law.
Sweet music from celestial isles
   Shall float across the azure seas,
And flowers, where endless summer smiles,
   Shall waft their perfumes on the breeze.

No empty void, no rayless night,
   No wintry waves by tempests tossed,
No treasures ravished from the sight,
   No blighted hopes, no blessing lost;

But all that was, or yet shall be,
   Through endless transformations led,
Shall know, through Life's sublime decree,
   A resurrection from the dead.

And he who, through the lapse of years,
   With aching heart and weary feet,
Had sought, from gloomy doubts and fears,
   A refuge and a sure retreat—
Shall find at last an inner shrine,
   Secure from superstition's ban,
Where he shall learn the truth divine,
   That God dwells evermore with man.

Throughout the boundless All in All,
   Life lengthens — an unbroken chain —
And He in whom we stand or fall,
   Feels all our pleasure and our pain.
O Infinite! O Holy Heart!
   Give us but patience to endure,
Until we know thee as thou art,
   And feel our lives in thee made sure.

GUARDIAN ANGELS.

Holy ministers of light!
Hidden from our mortal sight,
But whose presence can impart
Peace and comfort to the heart,
When we weep, or when we pray,
When we falter in the way,
Or our hearts grow faint with fear,
Let us feel your presence near.

Wandering over ways untrod,
Doubting self and doubting God,
Oft we miss the shining mark,
Oft we stumble in the dark.
Holy, holy life above!
Full of peace and perfect love,
Some sweet rays of summer shed
On the wintry ways we tread.

Blessed angels! ye who heed
All our striving, all our need,

When our eyes with weeping ache,
When our hearts in silence break,
When the cross is hard to bear,
When we fail to do and dare,
Make our wounded spirits feel
All your power to bless and heal.

When we gaze on new-made graves,
When the love the spirit craves,
Pure and saintly, like a star,
Shines upon us from afar,
Lead us *upward* to that light,
Till our faith is changed to sight,
Till we learn to murmur not,
And with patience bear our lot.

By our human weal and woe,
By our life of toil below,
By our sorrow and our pain,
By our hope of heavenly gain,
By these cherished forms of clay,
Fading from our sight away,
Do we plead for light, more light,
From that world beyond our sight.

Never, till our hearts are dust,
Till our souls shall cease to trust,

Till our love becomes a lie,
And our aspirations die,
Shall we cease with hope, to gaze
On that veil's mysterious haze,
Or the presence to implore
Of the loved ones gone before.

Holy spirit! quickening all,
On thy boundless love we call;
Send thy messengers of light,
To unseal our inward sight;
Lift us from our low estate,
Make us truly wise and great,
That our lives, through love, may be
Full of peace and rest in Thee.

NEARER TO THEE.

The following Poem was given at the conclusion of a lecture on "The Present Condition of Theodore Parker in Spirit Life"

> Nearer, my God, to Thee,
> Nearer to Thee.[1]

Yes, I *am* nearer Thee! for flesh and sense
   Have been exchanged for an eternal youth;
My spirit hath been born anew, and hence
   I worship Thee "in spirit and in truth."

Yes, I *am* nearer Thee! Though still unseen,
   Thy presence fills my life's diviner part.
Now that no earthly shadows intervene,
   I feel a deeper sense of what Thou art.

Yes, I *am* nearer Thee! Thy boundless love
   Fills all my being with a rich increase,
And soft descending, like a heavenly dove,
   I feel the benediction of Thy peace.

[1] The favorite hymn of Theodore Parker.

Yes, I *am* nearer Thee! All that I sought
 Of Truth, or Wisdom, or Eternal Right,
Is clearly present to my inmost thought,
 Like the uprising of a glorious light.

Yes, I *am* nearer Thee! O, calm and **still**,
 And beautiful and blest beyond degree,
Is this surrender of my finite will —
 Is this absorption of my soul in Thee.

"O Thou! whom men call God and know no
  more!"
When they shall leave the worship of the Past,
And learn to *love* Thee rather than *adore*,
 All souls shall draw thus near to Thee at last.

THE SACRAMENT.

The aged pastor broke the bread —
  With trembling hands he poured the wine —
"Eat — drink" — in earnest tones he said —
  "These emblems of a life divine —
His body broken for your sins;
  His blood for your salvation shed;
The priceless sacrifice that wins
  Life and redemption from the dead.

"See how with tender love he stands,
  And calls you to his faithful heart;
Lo! from his wounded side and hands
  Again the crimson life-drops start.
O sinner! wherefore will you stay,
  Regardless of your lost estate?
Come at your Saviour's call to-day,
  Before, alas! it is too late."

Forth from his lonely seat apart,
  A dark-browed, Ethiopian came,
As if new life had stirred the heart
  That beat within his manly frame.

"O, give to me," he meekly said,
  "A portion of that heavenly food;
I too would eat the living bread,
  And find salvation through his blood."

The Pastor turned with wondering eyes;
  But when he saw the dusky brow,
He answered, with a quick surprise,
  "Ho! bold intruder! Who art thou?
The master's table is not free
  To give the low-born servant place —
Such privilege can only be
  For his accepted sons of grace."

Upon the dusky brow there glowed
  A flush that was not wrath nor pride,
As forward he majestic strode,
  And stood close by the altar-side.
The broken bread his left hand spurned
  With sudden movement to the floor,
While with his right he quickly turned
  The consecrated chalice o'er.

One instant, for the tempest-cloud
  To gather on each pallid face.
And then uprose the angry crowd
  To thrust him from the sacred place.

With conscious might he raised his hand —
  A being of resistless will —
And uttered the sublime command
  That hushed the tempest — "Peace, be still!"

The waves of wrath and human pride
  Rolled back, without the power to harm,
The angry murmurs surged and died,
  And lo! there was a breathless calm.
The dusky brow to dazzling white
  Had in one fleeting instant turned,
And round his head a halo bright
  Of heaven's resplendent glory burned.

"I do reject," he calmly said,
  "These outward forms — this bread, this wine;
Lo! at *my* table *all* are fed,
  Made welcome by a love divine.
The high, the low, the rich, the poor,
  The black, the white, the bond, the free,
The sinful soul, the heart impure —
  Forbid them not to come to me.

"Too long, too long have faithless creeds
  Shut out the sunshine from above,
While human hearts, with human needs,
  Have perished from the lack of love.

O, break for them truth's living bread;
   Let love, like wine, unhindered flow;
Thus would I have the hungry fed,
   And let these outward emblems go."

Then from the altar-side there rose
   A cloud with matchless glory bright,
As when, at evening's calm repose,
   The sun withdraws his radiant light.
But though so far removed from all,
   He seemed in presence to depart,
The seed of living truth let fall
   Took root in many a thoughtful heart.

THE GOOD TIME NOW.

The world is strong with a mighty hope
  Of a good time yet to be,
And carefully casts the horoscope
  Of her future destiny;
And poet, and prophet, and priest, and sage,
  Are watching, with anxious eyes,
To see the light of that promised age
  On the waiting world arise.
O, weary and long seems that time to some,
  Who under Life's burdens bow,
For while they wait for that time to come,
  They forget 'tis a good time now.

Yes, a good time *now* — for we cannot say
  What the morrow will bring to view;
But we're always sure of the time to-day,
  And the course we must pursue;
And no better time is ever sought,
  By a brave heart, under the sun,
Than the present hour, with its noblest thought,
  And the duties to be done.

'Tis enough for the earnest soul to see
    There is work to be done, and how,
For he knows that the good time yet to be,
    Depends on the good time now.

There is never a broken link in the chain,
    And never a careless flaw,
For cause and effect, and loss and gain,
    Are true to a changeless law.
Now is the time to sow the seed
    For the harvest of future years,
Now is the time for a noble deed,
    While the need for the work appears.
You must earn the bread of your liberty
    By toil and the sweat of your brow,
And hasten the good time yet to be,
    By improving the good time now.

'Tis as bright a sun that shines to-day
    As will shine in the coming time;
And Truth has as weighty a word to say,
    Through her oracles sublime.
There are voices in earth, and air, and sky,
    That tell of the good time here,
And visions that come to Faith's clear eye,
    The weary in heart to cheer.

The glorious fruit on Life's goodly tree
    Is ripening on every bough,
And the wise in spirit rejoice to see
    The light of the good time now.

The world rests not, with a careless ease,
    On the wisdom of the past —
From Moses, and Plato, and Socrates,
    It is onward advancing fast;
And the words of Jesus, and John, and Paul,
    Stand out from the lettered page,
And the living present contains them all,
    In the spirit that moves the age.
Great, earnest souls, through the Truth made free,
    No longer in blindness bow,
And the good time coming, the yet to be,
    Has begun with the good time now.

Then up! nor wait for the promised hour,
    For the good time now is best,
And the soul that uses its gift of power
    Shall be in the present blest.
Whatever the future may have in store,
    With a will there is ever a way;
And none need burden the soul with more
    Than the duties of to-day.

Then up! with a spirit brave and free,
And put the hand to the plow,
Nor *wait* for the good time *yet to be*,
But *work* in the *good time now.*

LIFE'S MYSTERIES.

To the soul that is gifted with seeing
The secrets and sources of being,
    A mystical meaning appears
For the hearts that in silence are broken,
For the words of affection unspoken,
    For sorrow, bereavement, and tears.

There are souls that with genius are gifted,
On crosses of sorrow uplifted,
    Who find their salvation through pain;
There are deeds of the brave unrecorded,
And the toil of warm hands unrewarded,
    Whose loss is an infinite gain.

There are spirits who pray that no morrow
May dawn on the depths of their sorrow;
    But the morrow brings patience and peace.
And the faithful, who often with weeping

Have sown the good seed in their keeping,
　　Have garnered a blessed increase.

There are lives that are matchless in beauty,
Through the faithful performance of duty,
　　Whose labors of love are unknown.
There are spirits who languish in prison,
　　Whose light on the world has not risen,
　　And yet they are never alone.

The poor, the oppressed, and the lowly,
The selfish, the weak, and the holy,
　　Have each in life's drama a part.
While the wants and the woes that o'ercame them,
With the lives of the righteous who blame them,
　　Are known to the Infinite Heart.

O, where is the angel recorder!
And where is the watchman and warder,
　　That is charged with the keeping of souls?
And what is the mystical meaning,
Which the thoughtful in spirit are gleaning
　　From the Force that all Nature controls?

O, not where the sun-fires are burning,
And not where the planets are turning

Their faces to welcome the light,
Shall we seek for the Centre of Being,
And learn of the Wisdom All-seeing,
   Or climb to life's infinite hight.

But deep as love's fathomless ocean,
In a spirit of lowly devotion,
   Should we patiently strive to ascend;
Not reckless, unfeeling, and stoic,
But with courage and calmness heroic,
   Unswerving and true to the end.

With shoulders that bow to life's crosses,
With hearts that faint not at their losses,
   With spirits that triumph o'er pain, —
At length to such souls shall be given
The peaceful possession of heaven,
   And the life that is infinite gain.

Then, judged by the complex relation
Of each to the Soul of Creation,
   Distinctions of merit must fall.
There is good for the Saint and the Sinner,
There is gain for the loser or winner,
   And a just compensation for all.

For the Infinite Life is ascending,
And all things are with it uptending,
    Away from all evil and strife.
To man is the toil of endeavor,
But unto that Being, forever,
    The peace and perfection of life.

A WOODLAND IDYL.

OLD Brown Brier lived in the depths of a wood,
    Close down by a sassafras tree;
Jealous, and selfish, and hostile to all,
    A surly old fellow was he.
He hated his neighbor, the sassafras-tree,
    When her leaves grew green in the spring,
And he almost perished with envy and spite,
    When he heard an oriole sing.
But one thing saved him, and only one,
    From a life of sorrow and woe;
He longed for a change in his hermit life,
    And a power in himself to grow.

A fair young child to the green-wood came,
    With eyes like the gentian blue;
Her hair was like threads of an amber flame,
    And her cheek wore the sunset hue.
Her step was light as the bounding roe,
    And her voice like a silver bell;
She charmed the birds from their green retreats,
    And the squirrel from his cell.

She sang of the love, of the free, great love,
    Which the Father has for all,
From the worlds of light, in the heavens above,
    To the flowers and the insects small.

"Ah!" sighed the Brier, the brown old Brier,
    "What has he done for me?"
Does he give me leaves in the early spring,
    Or flowers like the locust tree?"

"Our God is just, and our God is true,"
    Still warbled the happy child;
"He sendeth his sunshine and silver dew
    To the desert and lonely wild;
And the secret force in the tempest cloud
    To the smallest flower is given,
That all, by his wisdom and strength endowed,
    May live for the Lord of Heaven."

She passed. The old Brier was lost in thought.
    "And is it, then, really so?
Can this wondrous change by *myself* be wrought?
    Have I power in myself to grow?"
Then up from the gray old mother Earth
    Rich juices he quickly drew,
Till the sluices and channels small were filled
    With the fresh sap trickling through.

He called to the winds, to the warm spring winds,
    As they played with the flowers near by,
And he prayed the sunshine, with golden wings,
    On his cold, damp roots to lie.
The spring winds blew, and the sunshine came,
    And the Brier grew fresh and fair,
Till his blossoms, like wreaths of incense cups,
    With their fragrance filled the air.

Again the child to the green-wood came;
    But her step was sad and slow;
Her eye beamed not with its love-lit flame,
    And her voice was soft and low.

"I am changed," she said; "O ye birds and flowers!
    With a yearning heart I weep
To lay me down in these quiet bowers,
    In a long, untroubled sleep.
For O, my heart like a flower is crushed,
    And I cling to the world no more;
The sacred fount from its urn hath gushed,
    And the joy of my life is o'er."

The summer winds through the green-wood passed,
    And the sweet Brier bowed his head;
A garland fair at her feet he cast,
    And in gentle tones he said, —

"Return to the world, dear child, return;
No longer *receive*, but *give!*
From a humble Brier this lesson learn:
Thou hast power in *thyself* to live.

JUBILATE.

Sung at the celebration of the 20th anniversary of Modern Spiritualism, March 31, 1868.

The world hath felt a quickening breath
   From Heaven's eternal shore,
And souls triumphant over Death
   Return to earth once more.
For *this* we hold our jubilee,
   For this with joy we sing —
"O Grave, where is thy victory?
   O Death, where is thy sting?"

Our cypress wreaths are laid aside
   For amaranthine flowers,
For Death's cold wave does not divide
   The souls we love from ours.
From pain, and death, and sorrow free,
   They join with us to sing —
"O Grave, where is thy victory?
   O Death, where is thy sting?"

Immortal eyes look from above
  Upon our joys to-night,
And souls immortal in their love
  In our glad songs unite.
Across the waveless crystal sea
  The notes triumphant ring —
"O Grave, where is thy victory?
  O Death, where is thy sting?"

"Sweet spirits, welcome yet again!"
  With loving hearts we cry;
And, "Peace on earth, good will to men,"
  The angel hosts reply.
From doubt and fear, through truth made free,
  With faith triumphant sing —
"O Grave, where is thy victory?
  O Death, where is thy sting?"

THE DIVINE IDEA.

When the morning came with her eyes of flame,
   And looked on the youthful earth;
When man, at the call of the Lord of All,
   Rose up in his glorious birth;
When the stars rang out, with a tuneful shout
   To the mountains and the sea,
And the world's great heart, with a quickened start,
   Beat time to their melody;—

Ere the dawning light in the heavens grew bright,
   Ere the march of the hours began,
God planted the seed of a mighty need,
   In the innermost soul of man.
'Twas the yearning wild that a little child
   For the fostering parent feels —
A holy thought with his life inwrought,
   Which his simplest act reveals.

The lion proud, like a servant, bowed
   At the might of his sovereign will;
But to man alone was the sense made known
   Of a power that was higher still.

Yet vague and dim was that thought to him;
    His simple and child-like mind
Could not gaze aright on that matchless light,
    So boundless and unconfined.

Gross by birth from his mother Earth,
    He needed some outward sign;
So the artisan planned, with a cunning hand,
    A *form* of the Great Divine.
And Baal, and Allah, and Juggernaut,
    And Brahma, and Zeus, and Pan,
Show how deeply wrought was that one great thought,
    In the worshiping soul of man.

Then his Deity came in the morning's flame,
    In the song of the sun-lit seas,
In the stars at night, in the noontide light,
    In the woods and the murmuring breeze.
To the Great Divine at the idol shrine,
    By each and by every name,
Through the fiery death or the prayerful breath,
    The worship was still the same.

Like a grain in the sod grew the thought of God,
    As Nature's slow work appears;
From the zoöphyte small, to the "Lord of all,"
    Through cycles and sums of years.

But the dark grew bright, and the night grew light,
   When the era of Truth began,
And the soul was taught, through its primal thought,
   Of the life of God in man.

Then the soul arose from her long repose,
   At the Truth's awakening breath,
And fearlessly trod as a child of God,
   Triumphant o'er Time and Death.
There came a sound from the wide world round,
   Like the surging of the sea,
Majestic and deep in its onward sweep —
   'Twas the anthem of the free.

Through the ages dim has that holy hymn
   Come down to our listening ears;
And still shall it float with a sweeter note
   Through the vista of coming years.
And a voice makes known from the viewless throne,
   "As it hath been, shall it be —
On! on from the past! still on to the last!
   Like a river that seeks the sea."

"Hour by hour, like an opening flower,
   Shall truth after truth expand;
The sun may grow pale, and the stars may fail,
   But the purpose of God shall stand.

Dogmas and creeds without kindred deeds,
   And altar and fane, shall fall;
One bond of love, and one home above,
   And one faith shall be to all."

THE PYRAMIDS.

"I was weary, very weary; but when I leaned against the Pyramids, they gave me strength." — KOSCIELSKI.

A WANDERER from his childhood's home,
   An exile from his father-land,
His weary feet were doomed to roam
   Far o'er the desert's scorching sand.
No mother o'er his pillow smiled,
   No sister's hand a blessing lent;
His only couch the desert wild,
   His only home an Arab tent.

Upon the classic shores of Greece,
   And by the imperial towers of Rome,
He vainly sought to find that peace
   Denied him in his childhood's home.
Beneath Lake Leman's watery bed,
   In Chillon's dungeon damp and low,
Communing with the mighty dead,
   His spirit felt a kindred glow.

He drank Circassia's breath of bloom,
    He climbed the Alps' eternal snows,
He plucked the leaves by Virgil's tomb,
    And stood where ancient Jordan flows.
And where Napoleon's falchion gleamed
    Along the borders of the Nile,
The pilgrim exile slept, and dreamed
    He saw his own loved mother's smile.

With weary feet he came, at last,
    Where, all untouched by Time's rude hands,
The Pyramids their shadows cast
    Upon the desert's burning sands.
Still in their works of greatness dwelt
    The spirits of these mighty men;
Before their majesty he knelt!
    He rose — and he was strong again.

O thou! whose life is all inwrought
    With cheerful faith and strength sublime,
Leave *thou* some monumental thought
    Upon the desert waste of Time.
Some exile from his native heaven
    May tread the path which thou hast trod,
And through *thy works* may strength be given
    To lift his spirit up to God.

THE INNER MYSTERY.

The following inspirational poem was delivered at a festival commemorative of the twentieth anniversary of the advent of Modern Spiritualism, held in Music Hall, Boston, March 31, 1868.

It is an allegorical description of the progress of a soul from the Valley of Superstition and Traditional Theology to the highest mountain peaks of Natural Philosophy and Spiritual Revelation. He is strengthened and encouraged in his progress by the voices "of the loved ones gone before." At length, in the higher regions of metaphysical reasoning and abstract philosophy, he encounters the demon Doubt — a representative of popular Theology and traditional authority. This Doubt endeavors to make him distrust reason, and render a blind credence to mere authority. In the struggle with the demon the great Truth flashes with a realizing sense upon the soul, that by its inherent nature *it is older than all forms of Truth, and one with God himself.* In the strength of this conviction he conquers, and the demon is slain.

Thus " THE INNER MYSTERY " is revealed, and the unfolding of the spiritual perceptions follows as a legitimate result.

"According to Fichte, there is a Divine Idea pervading the visible universe; which visible universe is indeed but its symbol and sensible manifestation, having in itself no meaning, or even true existence, independent of it. To the mass of men this Divine Idea lies hidden; yet to discern it, to seize it, and live wholly in it, is the condition of all genuine virtue, knowledge, freedom, and the end, therefore, of all spiritual effort in every age." — CARLYLE.

In the valley, where the darkness
  Dropped its poisonous vapors on my head,
Where the night winds moaned and murmured,
  Like the voices of the troubled dead,
    Groping, stumbling, weary and alone,
  Did I make the earth my bed,
    And my pillow was a stone.

    O, that slumber!
It was long, and dark, and deep,
Till a voice cried, "Come up hither!"
And I started from my sleep.

"Whither?" cried I; and it answered,
  "Come up hither! for the day is dawning;
Through the gates of amethyst and amber
  Shines the kindling glory of the morning."

    Gazing upward,
I beheld assurance of the day;
    Hopeful-hearted,
O'er the mountain-path I took my way.
    'Mid the pine trees
Did I hear life's drowsy pulses start,
    Swinging, singing,
Making sweet, but mournful music,
    Thrilling, filling,
All the lonely places of my heart.

Then the embers of the morning,
　　Smouldering on night's funeral pyre,
Kindling into sudden brightness,
　　Lit the mountain-peaks with fire;
And the quickened heart of Nature
　　Answered from her Memnon lyre.
Eager, earnest, still ascending,
　　Toward the glories of the day,
I could hear that voice my steps attending,
With the matin-hymn of Nature blending,
Ever crying, "Come up hither!"
　　And I followed in the way.

Bright the sky glowed with celestial splendor,
　　Like the light of love from God's own eyes;
And the lofty mountains seemed to tender
　　Back their crowns of glory to the skies.
　　　　Far above me,
　　In the hights so terrible and grand,
　　　　I could see the glaciers gleaming
　　In the hollow of the mountain's hand.
　　　　Flashing, dashing,
　　From the steeps the foaming cataract poured,
　　　　Over pathways
　　Which the mighty avalanche had scored.
　　　　Dim and ghostly
　　Rose the silvery clouds of wreathéd spray,

Rainbow-mantled,
Vanishing in upper air away.
Elfin shadows
O'er my lonely pathway leaped and played,
As the pine trees
Dreamily their murmuring branches swayed.
All the air seemed filled with voices,
Which I ne'er had thought to hear again;
And I fled, to leave behind me,
Sounds of pleasure close allied to pain.
Upward, onward, did I speed my way,
Nearer to the perfect source of day.
Awed by beauty and by terror,
Tearful, prayerful, did I sink,
Where the tender, blue-eyed gentian
Bloomed upon the glacier's brink.

"Save me! O thou loving Lord!" I cried,
"From the unforeseen intrusion
Of this sad, but sweet delusion,
From this strange and cruel semblance
To the cherished love that long since died.

"Come up hither!"
Cried my unknown guide who went before.
"Come up hither!"
And I followed in the way once more,—

THE INNER MYSTERY.

Upward, where the tempests gathered,
Where the lightnings crouched within their lair,
Where the mighty God of thunder
With his hammer smote the shuddering air,
Where the tall cliffs, battle-splintered,
Reared their lofty summits, bleak and bare;
Higher yet, where all my life-tide,
With the breath of Heaven grew chill;
And I felt my pulses quickened,
With a strange, electric thrill.

Not one blossom brightened in my pathway,
Not one lichen dared that wintry breath;
But far up above, and all around me,
Brooded awful silence, as of death.
And I walked where ragged precipices,
Overhanging wild and dark abysses,
Frowned upon the dizzy depths below;
Where the yawning chasms,
Rent by earthquake spasms,
Strove to fill their hungry throats with snow.
Burdened with a sense of solemn grandeur,
With a deeply reverent heart I trod
'Mid those awful and majestic altars
Of the Unknown God.

Musing deeply,
As I turned an angle of the rocky wall,
Lo! before me
Stood a figure, ghostly, gaunt, and tall;
Like the famous, fabled image,
Falling from Dardanian skies,
Wrapped in white, marmorial silence,
Did he greet my wondering eyes.

Straight upon the narrow pathway,
Fixed as fate, he seemed to stand,
With a widely yawning chasm,
And a wall on either hand.

"Come up hither! come up hither!"
Cried the voice that went before;
And my spirit leaped impatient
To obey the call once more.

"Let me pass, I pray thee,"
Said I in a calm and courteous tone;
But he only gazed upon me,
With a face as passionless as stone.

"Prithee, stand aside!" I said more firmly,
"For I may not stay;
I must reach the mountain-hights above me
Ere the close of day."

But he stirred not, spake not, breathed not,
  Only turned his stony eyes
Downward — to the yawning chasm,
  Upward — to the distant skies.

    "Wherefore," said I,
  With a slowly kindling wrath,
"Do you seek to stay my progress,
  Do you stand across my path?
What am I to thee, or thou to me?
  Stand aside, or prithee, sirrah,
Which is stronger we shall shortly see.

Like a statue did he stand — the same.
Then my smothered wrath waxed hotter;
"Demon! speak thy name and tell thine errand!"
Cried I, with a loudly ringing shout;
And his cold lips parted, as he answered,
    "I am Doubt.

    "Go no farther,
For a phantom lures thee on thy way;
    Upward striving
Will not bring thee nearer to the perfect day.
    In the valley
All is warmth, and rest, and kindly cheer;
    Go no farther;
It is *lone* and *very cold up here.*

"Trust not to your erring Reason
All your aspirations to control;
  Man grows ripe before the season
  When he heeds the promptings of the soul.

"Come up hither! come up hither,"
  Cried the tuneful voice again;
"Doubt should never counsel duty,
  When the way of truth is plain.

"Stay!" replied the watchful demon;
  "Thou *shalt* lend an ear to Doubt,
  For, by Heaven! thou shalt not pass me
  Until thou hast heard me out.
Thou art deeply cursed from the beginning,
All thy nature is corrupt with sinning;
God refuses thee his grace to-day;
Christ alone his righteous wrath can stay.
  All thy prayerful aspiration
  But retards thy soul's salvation;
All the efforts of thy godless will
Make thy deep damnation deeper still.
  O thou self-deluded dreamer!
  O thou transcendental schemer!
  Leave thine idle speculations,
  Trances, visions, exaltations,
And thy toilsome upward progress stay.

By thy fallen, lost condition,
By the depths of thy perdition,
    I have promised,
Yea, have *sworn*, to turn thee from this way.

"Come up hither! come up hither!"
Cried the voice persuasive from above.
    Then I looked, and bending o'er me,
I beheld my long-lost angel love.

"Back!" I shouted to the demon.
"Never!" in a measured tone he said,
    "Till the final resurrection,
Till the earth and sea give up their dead."

        Then I smote him —
Smote him in the forehead and the eyes;
        And I shouted,
"I will not be cozened by your lies!
        Go to cowards
With your Hebrew husks and pious pelf,
For MY SOUL IS OLDER THAN THE TRUTH,
    ONE WITH GOD HIMSELF."

Then my blows fell fiercer, harder, hotter,
        Till he yielded
Like the clay-formed vessel of a potter;

And I crashed into his brainless skull,
　　Smote his stony eyes out, cold and dull;
Into shards amorphous dashed his lips profane,
　　And, as brittle as a bubble,
　　　　Clove his shattered trunk in twain.
　　Then, as if God's mill-stones surely
　　　　Had been given me in trust,
　　On the rock I stood securely,
　　　　And those fragments ground to dust.

But, O, God! what wondrous transformation
　　Seized me in its mighty grasp of power!
As a bud, by Nature's potent magic,
　　Bursts at once into a perfect flower!
Like the record of a wise historian,
　　Lay unsealed the wondrous Book of Life;
Swelling grandly, like a chant Gregorian,
　　Perfect unison arose from strife;
And I knew then that this grim, defiant elf,
That this clay-born image, was my weaker self;
That this demon, Doubt, with which I held such
　　　　strife,
Was the sense's logic — the phenomena of life;
And as Perseus slew the fabled Gorgon,
Must this mocking fiend be met and slain,
That transfixed in cold and stony silence
Faith and Hope no longer might remain.

Only when the conscious soul asserted
  What the flesh and sense so long concealed,
GOD WITHIN — ONE WITH THE WEAK AND HUMAN,
  Did the INNER MYSTERY stand revealed.
O, what glorious consummation to my strife!
Death of Death! and Life unto Eternal Life!
All around, the grand and awful mountains
Hushed in silent reverence seemed to stand,
      White and shining,
Like the pearly portals of the better land.
  Then I heard the angels singing,
    Soft and clear the sweet notes ringing,
Dropping gently like a golden rain
    From the treasured wealth of day;
And I caught these words of blessing,
    Floating down the heavenly way: —

SONG OF THE ANGELS.

"O, what is the life of the soul,
But the life of the Infinite Whole?
    For God and his creatures are One,
As the tide from the ocean of light,
Which sets through the day and the night,
    Is the same in the star-beam or sun.

"He hath laid out the sea and the land;
He hath balanced the Heavens in his hand;

And the Earth, in that order sublime,
How greatly and grandly she rolls,
And casts off her harvests of souls,
  In the boundless fruition of Time!

"We ask not his face to behold;
Of his glory we need not be told;
  For the Word of his witness is near.
His Life is the Infinite Light,
Which quickens our blindness to sight;
  And he speaks that his children may hear.

"He suffers and sins with them all;
He stands, or he falls when they fall;
  For he is both substance and breath.
Their strength from his greatness they draw;
His wisdom and will are their law;
  And he is their Saviour in death.

"When the depths of all hearts are unsealed
Shall the word of his truth be revealed,
  That MAN is by NATURE DIVINE;
And faith in God's presence within,
Shall strengthen the spirit to win
  A peace which no tongue can define."

Then the music floated upward,
   Where the light of parting day,
With its gold and crimson glory,
   On the mountain summits lay;
And it left me longing, praying,
And with quickened steps essaying
   Swift the nearest hights to gain,
That my captivated being
Might unto a clearer seeing
   Of those fading forms attain.
And ere long, with hands uplifted,
   Kneeling on the mountain high,
Out into the listening silence
   Did I send my pleading cry:—
"O thou beauteous land of Beulah,
   Just beyond my longing sight!
O ye bright ones, loved and lovely,
   Dwelling in celestial light!
Leave, O! leave me not behind you
   With the darkness and the night!"
In the sunshine and the shadow,
   Then I saw an open door;
And a voice cried, "Come up hither!
   Life is yours forevermore."
Gales of Araby around me
   Seemed to wave their fragrant wings;
Strains of music, low and tender,
   Thrilled along celestial strings.

Like a spotless lily, blending
  Matchless bloom and breath divine,
Did my lost one, long lamented,
  Lay her soft white hand in mine;
    And uplifted,
    Strangely gifted,
With a power unknown before,
Did my love and I together
  Enter at the open door.

Lo! again those bright immortals,
  As their fadeless flowers they wreathe,
Words of greeting oft repeating,
  Celebrate this festive eve.
Listen to their tuneful message
  For the hearts that joy or grieve:—

Song of the Ministering Spirits.

"Truth's heralds bright,
  With feet of light,
Upon Life's mountains stand,
  Sent to proclaim,
  In God's high name,
Glad tidings to the land.
  With smiles of love
  They wait above,

And, 'Come up hither!' cry.
    When souls shall climb
    Life's hights sublime,
Then Death itself shall die.

"The little child,
    Whose bright eyes smiled,
Whom angel-hands upbore,
    The good, the kind,
    The pure in mind,
Glide through Life's open door.
    With voices sweet,
    Their lips repeat
The chorus of the sky: —
    'All souls shall be
    From doubt made free,
And Death itself shall die.'

"Joy crowns with flowers
    Life's summer-hours,
When storms of sorrow cease;
    And wintry snows,
    And calm repose,
Bring thoughts of holy peace.
    Thus pales or burns
    Life's star by turns,

As swift the moments fly;
But winter's blight,
And sorrow's night,
And Death itself, shall die.

"From Death's abyss
To hights of bliss
Must souls immortal strive;
While loss and gain,
And peace and pain,
Shall keep their faith alive.
But higher still,
With tireless will,
Their course shall upward lie,
Till palms shall wave
Above the grave,
And Death itself shall die."

www.ingramcontent.com/pod-product-compliance
Lightning Source LLC
Chambersburg PA
CBHW032222230426
43666CB00033B/681